I CAN
right angle weave

I CAN

Mabeline Gidez

right angle weave

From Basic Stitch to
Advanced Techniques,
**A COMPREHENSIVE
WORKBOOK FOR BEADERS**

LARK CRAFTS
Asheville

EDITOR
Nathalie Mornu

TECHNICAL EDITOR
Bonnie Brooks

EDITORIAL ASSISTANCE
Dawn Dillingham
Hannah Doyle

ART DIRECTOR
Kathleen Holmes

ART PRODUCTION
Kay Holmes Stafford

JUNIOR DESIGNER
Carol Morse Barnao

ILLUSTRATORS
How to: Mabeline Gidez
Difficulty levels: J'aime Allene

PHOTOGRAPHER
Stewart O'Shields

BOOK & COVER DESIGNER
Laura Palese

EDITORIAL INTERN
Alex Alesi

An Imprint of Sterling Publishing
387 Park Avenue South
New York, NY 10016

If you have questions or comments about
this book, please visit: larkcrafts.com

Library of Congress Cataloging-in-Publication Data

Gidez, Mabeline.
  I CAN Right Angle Weave : From Basic Stitch to Advanced Techniques,
a Comprehensive Workbook for Beaders / Mabeline Gidez. -- First Edition.
    pages cm
  Includes index.
  ISBN 978-1-4547-0366-2
  1. Beadwork--Patterns. 2. Weaving--Patterns. 3. Jewelry making. I. Title.
  TT860.G49 2012
  745.594'2--dc23
                          2012005448

10 9 8 7 6 5 4 3 2 1

First Edition

Published by Lark Crafts
An Imprint of Sterling Publishing Co., Inc.
387 Park Avenue South, New York, NY 10016

Text © 2012, Mabeline Gidez
Photography © 2012, Lark Crafts, an Imprint of Sterling Publishing Co., Inc.,
unless otherwise specified
Illustrations © 2012, Mabeline Gidez

Distributed in Canada by Sterling Publishing,
c/o Canadian Manda Group, 165 Dufferin Street
Toronto, Ontario, Canada M6K 3H6

Distributed in the United Kingdom by GMC Distribution Services,
Castle Place, 166 High Street, Lewes, East Sussex, England BN7 1XU

Distributed in Australia by Capricorn Link (Australia) Pty Ltd.,
P.O. Box 704, Windsor, NSW 2756 Australia

Manufactured in China

978-1-4547-0366-2

For information about custom editions, special sales, premium, and
corporate purchases, please contact the Sterling Special Sales Department
at 800-805-5489, or specialsales@sterlingpub.com.

Submit requests for information about desk and examination copies
available to college and university professors to academic@larkbooks.com.
Our complete policy can be found at www.larkcrafts.com.

contents

introduction

I first turned to beading as a creative, stress-relieving outlet in college. Like a meditation that cleared my mind of everything, beading was a special "me" time where I could focus on the pretty, sparkly jewels at my fingertips. Beading classes didn't exist then, so I learned from books. I've come a long way since.

One stitch stumped me from the very beginning—right angle weave, also known as RAW. No matter how I tried, I simply couldn't wrap my brain around it. It didn't help that early books and magazines didn't present RAW well. Several steps were usually combined into one diagram, resulting in a maze with so many overlapping thread paths that I couldn't find my way. I wanted one drawing to see how to make the first unit, a second one to understand where to position my thread for the next unit, a third describing how to attach the next unit, and so forth. Frustrated, I just gave up.

A few years later, I tackled RAW again. If other people could do it, so could I! After a while, it just clicked, and I discovered that RAW was the most versatile of stitches and could create so many different designs.

This is the book I wanted when I first started. It doesn't tell you how to bead—it shows you. I don't rely on words and a few diagrams to get the idea across. Instead, I break everything down into simple steps supplemented by illustrations with easy-to-follow thread paths. Especially in the beginner projects, I provide diagrams for almost every step, which guarantees your success. For experienced beaders, this book provides a comprehensive refresher course for true excellence with the stitch.

Each chapter focuses on a single skill, providing the building blocks for subsequent sections. Projects start easy and progress to intermediate, so you gain a better understanding of the technique. I begin with the fundamentals of RAW with a chapter that includes four simple projects. For example, the Sassy Stripes Tennis Bracelet is completely straightforward, but bands of colored beads add a level of skill building.

Once you've gotten the hang of the basic stitch, move on to the next chapter to learn increasing and decreasing and to stretch and strengthen your beading brainpower. The Hearts Aflutter Earrings offer a fun, easy way to create a shape that's not square or rectangular. Later chapters show how to embellish over and around RAW, how to curve it, going tubular, and a variation called polygon or triangle stitch. The final chapter teaches beaded beads. The sparkling Lantern Bead Necklace is a gorgeous example.

If you've ever been too intimidated by RAW, here's your chance to start fresh! Take things slow. Explore your creative potential, and—most important—have a blast learning, beading, and building your skills! Now you can right angle weave!

materials & tools

As a beading instructor, I have the pleasure of interacting with lots of talented people in the beading world, and I get exposed to many types of beads and beading supplies. Although I haven't had a chance to try every product, I have managed to sample my fair share of what's out there. The thread, beads, needle sizes, and so on that you choose to work with depend on the type of project you're making. I believe that every bead, thread, and tool has its purpose.

BEADS

Beads, beautiful beads! So many colors, so many choices!

Seed Beads

Seed beads are small, with rounded edges. They look like little seeds and come in many sizes denoted with an ott symbol, or °. The larger the number, the smaller the bead. A size 8° is much larger than an 11°, and an 11° is twice the size of a 15°. There are two types of seed beads: Czech seed beads, which are often sold in hanks (strands already prestrung with beads), and Japanese seed beads, which are sold loosely by the gram.

There are two main differences between Czech and Japanese seed beads. Japanese seed beads are more uniform in shape and size, and they have larger bead holes than the Czech seed beads. This is why I prefer to use Japanese seed beads over Czech beads. There's nothing worse than not being able to pass the needle through a bead because the bead hole is completely filled with thread too soon!

Cylinder Beads

Cylinder beads come in myriad colors. They're perfect for beadweaving because their dimensions are always uniform, the edges are very straight (unlike round-edged seed beads), and their bead holes are quite roomy. Although they come in several sizes (once again, the higher the number, the smaller the bead), the most popular size to work with is size 11°.

Triangle Beads

Triangle beads have three sides and come in several sizes, too. Some have pointed edges, while others are more rounded. The edges almost look faceted, so these beads are excellent for embellishing. They can give a piece wonderful texture! Again, the larger the size number, the smaller the bead.

Drop Beads

Teardrop shaped with a hole at the tip, drop beads come in a few sizes and many colors. They're great for adding a bubbling texture to beadwork and for the fringes typically added to lariat-style necklaces, heavily embellished bracelets, and amulet bags.

Glass Beads

Glass beads come in all shapes, sizes, and colors. Unlike seed beads, these are measured in millimeters. For the projects in this book, I include only commonly available fire-polished beads and glass daggers.

The term "fire-polished bead" derives from a two-part manufacturing process. After creating faceted, round glass beads, the manufacturer briefly reheats them to polish away the rough edges. Although they're available in several shapes, the projects in this book call only for round fire-polished beads.

Glass daggers are spear shaped with the hole drilled at the top. They come in several sizes, colors, and patterns. I just love the daggers with dots on them! Dagger beads are commonly used for embellishing and for fringe on necklaces and beaded amulet bags.

Crystals

Crystals are my favorite bead to work with. Their sparkle rivals the stars in the sky, making them irresistible to most beaders. Several companies manufacture crystals. The variety of shapes, sizes, and colors is impossible to keep up with! The consistency of size and color of Austrian crystals sets them apart from those produced elsewhere and makes them the top choice among beaders. Other crystals aren't as perfect and sparkly, but they offer much cheaper and perfectly acceptable alternative if the size and shape of the bead isn't imperative to the project. The only downside to crystals is the sharp edges that can cut most types of thread.

THREAD

All threads, except for braided beading thread, need to be stretched prior to beading. Pre-stretching your thread reduces the amount of stretching in your beadwork over time. It also helps improve how tight your beads sit together. Stretching thread is simple: Hold a section of thread between two hands and pull with moderate force. Repeat with the next section of thread. I usually pull 2 to 3 feet (61 to 91.4 cm) at a time. Don't pull with all your strength or you might snap the thread.

TIP: I'm often asked what color thread to use for a given project. If the brand only comes in dark gray or white, I choose white when working with lightly colored or transparent beads, and gray for dark or opaque-colored beads. If the thread comes in a variety of colors, then I suggest using a thread color that brings out the shade of your beads. Thread not only keeps your beads woven together, but it can also enhance your beadwork.

Nymo

Nymo thread is a nylon beading thread that comes in many different colors. It's much stronger than cotton thread and is commonly used in both loom and off-loom beadwork. Nymo comes in many thicknesses, ranging from OO (thinnest) to F (thickest). The most commonly used thickness is size D. Certain projects—but none in this book—may specify size B if they use lots of beads with small holes and require lots of thread to go through them. Nymo thread from a small bobbin has more stretch than Nymo from a bobbin or cone. Be aware that there's a risk of splitting Nymo with a needle. Splitting thread weakens it.

Silamide

This twisted two-ply nylon beading thread only comes in one size, but in a good selection of colors. Because the thread is twisted, it's a little difficult to thread into the eye of a thin needle. It feels a little thicker than Nymo size D thread and other threads. Unlike Nymo, splitting Silamide doesn't happen frequently and is not as problematic. I typically don't reach for this thread when working with really small beads or when working with lots of crystals.

Braided Beading Thread

Braided beading thread was originally marketed and used as fishing line. It was quickly adopted by beaders, however, when we discovered how well it performed with crystals and sharp-edged beads! Several manufacturers produce it. Unlike the threads previously described, this one is more resilient. However, it's not completely indestructible, and once in a blue moon I've split it with my needle. It's somewhat wiry and gives your beadwork a stiffer feel. This thread doesn't come in a variety of colors like the others. You'll typically find it in either smoke gray or crystal white. Cut it with a sharp pair of children's scissors.

The packaging of the thread denotes its size and/or test weight. Test weight shows how strong the thread is—the higher the weight, the stronger the thread, which also means the thread will be thicker. For beading, a good size to have is size D or 6-pound test weight. I also use size B or 4-pound test weight in projects that have beads with small holes and require lots of passes through those holes.

TIP: You can lightly tint white braided beading thread with a permanent marker. Choose a color darker than what you want because the thread won't fully absorb the ink. After coloring, let the ink dry for a few seconds before beading. I haven't had any problems with the color bleeding onto my skin when I wear the finished piece, but a little bit of ink may stain your fingers as you bead.

One G

This relatively new nylon beading thread from Japan is pretreated with a thin coating to prevent tangling. It comes in a variety of colors and, though similar to Nymo size D thread, it's a little bit stronger. It's not as strong as braided beading thread when it comes to crystals, however, so be wary.

K.O.

A nylon beading thread that comes in a variety of colors, K.O., like One G, also hails from Japan. It's similar to Nymo size B but is prewaxed and a little bit stronger. Like many of the other nylon threads, it gives your beadwork a nice, supple feel. You're less likely to split this thread with a needle, but I've had problems with K.O. breaking when used with crystals, so I reserve it for smooth-edged beads only.

Conditioning Thread

Before starting a project, I like to coat my thread to enhance it, for the reasons described below. As you pull the thread through beads, eventually the coating wears off, so multiple applications will be required.

Thread Heaven reduces the risk of tangling, and it makes the thread a little slippery, so taking out a knot is a little easier. This product is ideal for beadwork that you want to remain soft and supple like fabric. It comes in a little blue box. I hold the thread over the gel-like texture inside and pull it through twice.

Wax gives the thread a tacky coating that makes the beads stick together when woven. The benefits are that your beadwork will be stiffer and the tension will be a little tighter. This is ideal for sculptural pieces such as beaded beads. Beeswax tends to be a little bit crumbly and doesn't coat the thread as well as microcrystalline wax does, which is my favorite because it's sold in a big chunk and coats the thread more smoothly.

Carve out a small piece with a spoon and keep it in a small zip-top bag. Warm up the little ball of wax in your hands and then glide the thread through it. The warmed wax coats the thread better and leaves little to no lumps.

CLASPS

Like beads, you'll find many types of clasps out there. The colors are limited to silver, gold, copper, and brass. There are clasps for one-strand, two-strand, three-strand, and more jewelry. There are sliding bar clasps in several widths depending on how many strands you need to connect to. While attaching these to your beadwork, it's best to leave them clasped. Magnetic sliding bar clasps are the easiest to put on and take off but are priced a little higher.

Then there are toggle clasps. These have a ring on one end and a bar on the other. When picking one out, test it first if possible. Pass the bar through the loop to see whether you'll have difficulty with it. Be wary if the bar is too short; it may easily fall out of the loop end when worn.

Box-style clasps are the most decorative. One clasp end is a folded tab of metal that feeds into a slot in the other half. Over time, the folded tab won't hold as well in the slot and you risk losing your piece.

With ball-and-socket clasps, you pop a ball end into a round socket end until you hear a snap. That sound indicates the clasp is closed and secure. Be wary! Try them out first before purchasing. Sometimes the ball isn't well soldered and can pop off its base. These clasps are available in two sizes. Anything 6 mm or smaller may be hard to handle. In this case, bigger is better!

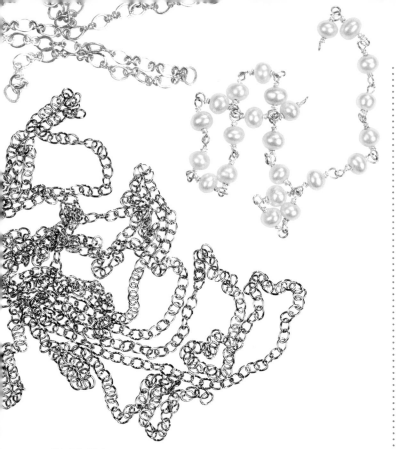

CHAIN

Chain is usually sold by the foot and comes in a variety of styles. When shopping for it, pay attention to the size of the links. Small links are more delicate than bigger, heavier ones. Sometimes chain is priced by weight. In this case, heavier chain will cost more. Some chains have beads already wire wrapped together, which saves time.

For chain with small links, a ruler and a needle make things easier. Measure out one length of chain and cut it with wire cutters. Slide the piece of chain onto a needle. Hang the rest of the chain from the same needle and use the first piece as a guide to see how much to cut off.

> **TIP:** When cutting several pieces of chain that need to be the same length, if the chain has large links, measure and cut the first segment and count its links. The other lengths of chain should have the same number of links—no need to measure.

WIRE AND HEAD PINS

When you need to connect elements in this book, you may use wire to make a link. Wire comes in different thicknesses known as gauges. The higher the gauge number, the thinner the wire. Choose somewhere

between 22- and 26-gauge round wire. (If you're using chain with very small links, then 26 gauge is ideal.) Dangles call for head pins, a commercial finding that consists of a short length of wire with a flattened end that prevents beads that are strung on from falling off.

EARRING FINDINGS

When you make earrings, you need earring findings to attach them to your ears. Posts, hooks, lever-backs, and clip-ons are all fine, but they must have a small loop at the base so that you can attach things to them.

Wire Guards/Protectors

Wire guards, also known as wire protectors, are U-shaped tubes with an exposed channel in the middle used to protect the stringing material from abrasion. They give a nice finish to beadwork, as shown in the Sunny Flowers Earrings (page 97).

JUMP RINGS

An open jump ring has a gap or open seam that allows the ring to be opened with pliers. When attaching beadwork directly to a jump ring, it's imperative to use a closed jump ring, the ends or seam of which are soldered closed, leaving no gap for the thread to pass through. No matter how closely you match the ends of an open jump ring, the thread could still slip through the seam and your jewelry might fall apart.

TOOLS AND MISCELLANEOUS

For the projects in this book, you need only a few specialized tools.

Needles

Needles must be skinny enough to pass through the holes in beads. Beading needles are available in all sorts of sizes. The thickest beading needle commonly used is a size 10. Beaders like this size because it won't bend and has the largest eye, making it easier to thread. As their size increases, needles become thinner, with a smaller eye. Thinner needles bend more easily. Really tense beaders who hold them tightly tend to curve them into C shapes. Some recently introduced thinner needles won't bend, but I still prefer longer, thinner needles because their flexibility allows me to get into tight areas, and the length allows me to add many beads onto the needle.

The size of the needle to use depends on the type of beads in the project. Because I tend to use small beads in my designs, I prefer size 12 or size 13 beading needles. With good lighting and good glasses, I'm able to get a size D thread through the eye.

Beading Mats

Beads tend to roll around, especially when you're trying to pick them up onto your needle. Some beaders hold their beads in little ceramic dishes with divided sections, while others use a tray with a velvet pad insert. I prefer a piece of velour fabric (the kind blankets are made of). Bead stores sell these in a variety of colors. It's tempting to buy one in your favorite color, but bear in mind that light-colored beads show up well on a darker fabric while darker beads are more visible against lighter colored fabric. If you tend to use a lot of purple in your beaded jewelry, opt for a light pink or cream-colored fabric instead of dark blue or purple.

Scissors

Personally, I use scissors from the scrapbooking/paper crafting section at my craft store. Some fancy scissors designed for sewing work well on nylon beading threads. These threads are gentle enough not to dull the scissors immediately. However, cut braided beading thread with children's scissors. Whichever scissors you choose to use, reserve them only for cutting thread. This will increase the longevity of your scissors.

Thread Burner

When trimming excess thread off beadwork, scissors always leave behind a small piece of thread sticking out, which I call thread stubble. Burners or zappers have a metal tip that gets hot and melts the end of any nylon or other synthetic thread; the thread melts and shrinks into the beadwork and you don't get thread stubble. Nifty! Use burners only when trimming thread from beadwork, not for cutting thread from a spool.

Thread Bobbins

In some of the projects, a portion of thread is saved for later use. I suggest you wrap it onto a bobbin so it doesn't tangle. Some beaders use a piece of cardboard or paper instead. You can also find plastic bobbin cards, which are sturdier, but the thread is still prone to unraveling. I prefer the small plastic bobbins used for kumihimo (a Japanese form of braid making). They look like toy yo-yos but really keep the thread secure. To use, flip one side up to expose the spool inside. Wrap on the thread. Fold the top back down to hold the wrapped thread.

Measuring Tape

Whether you need to measure a length of thread or figure out how long a necklace to weave, a measuring tape is necessary.

Tools for Wire Wrapping

You're probably wondering why wire-wrapping tools are covered in a book about beading. Who says you can't incorporate a little chain and wire wrapping into beadwork? I love mixing things up!

Chain-nose pliers for jewelry making are different than pliers sold in the hardware store because they're smaller, are smooth on the inside, and the nose tapers down to a narrow point. You'll use them to grasp wire and make bends or angles.

Round-nose pliers for jewelry making also have a nose that tapers down to a narrow point. The difference is

TIP: To make identical-looking loops consistent in size, use a fine-point permanent marker to mark the place on the round-nose pliers where you want to wrap the loops, and always work on that spot. (I make my mark approximately 3 mm from the tip for small loops and 5 mm from the tip for medium-size loops.)

that round-nose pliers are rounded on the inside, not flat. Their purpose is for making loops. Use the tip of the pliers for small loops, and work higher up on the wider section of the pliers to make bigger loops.

Flush cutters are essential for wire wrapping. One side is smooth, letting you snip the wire close to your work with a nice blunt cut. Use flush cutters for cutting wire only!

basic flat RAW

· · · · · · · · · · · · · · · ·

The right angle weave stitch (or RAW for short) is a series of units that, when connected together, form a grid. In traditional RAW, the units are in the shape of squares. The angles of the square are 90°, or right angles, hence the name of the stitch. In later projects, you'll discover that the stitch isn't confined only to right angles.

The units are woven either clockwise or counterclockwise. These units have a top, a bottom, a left side, and a right side. In a row of RAW, the units share their left and right sides. A good analogy is to imagine adding a new room to a house. The house and new room share a wall, or a side.

To begin, use a pair of sharp scissors to cut a piece of thread. In general, a comfortable amount of thread is 36 to 72 inches (91.4 cm to 1.8 m) long. The disadvantage of using short pieces of thread is that you'll eventually have to weave in new

thread when the one on the needle is too short to keep using. I know how unhappy most beaders are about adding new threads, and that's why I design my projects with reasonable thread lengths, and with the addition of new threads as part of the process.

Next, depending on the project, condition the thread with either wax or thread conditioner. Wax is ideal for beaded bead projects in chapter 8, while thread conditioner like Thread Heaven is preferred for supple beadwork like the Sweet Lattice Bracelet (page 23). I prefer using single

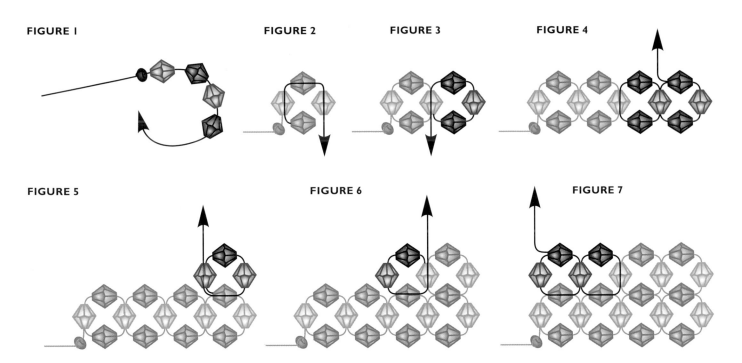

FIGURE 1   FIGURE 2   FIGURE 3   FIGURE 4

FIGURE 5   FIGURE 6   FIGURE 7

thread because it's easier to undo a mistake and the bead holes won't fill up too quickly. That's what you should do in all of this book's projects as well.

Figures 1 through 4 show the progression of how to create the first row of RAW. This row consists of four units. To make the first unit, string four crystals—each crystal represents one side. The purple crystals are the top and bottom of the unit. The topaz crystals are the left and right sides of the unit. For the second unit (figure 3), only three crystals are added because one crystal is shared between the first and second unit.

When creating a new row above the previous one, the units in the rows share either the top or the bottom, or both if there are several rows stacked on top of each other. Think of a row as a floor or level in a building. The ceiling of the first level is the bottom floor of the second level. Figures 5 through 7 show the progression of how the second row is created. The first unit of the second row is the only unit that requires three new crystals. The rest of the units in this row need only two new crystals each. Figure 7 image shows a completed second row with a total of four units.

RAW can be done with either one needle or two. (Most of the projects in this book are made with one needle. Pearly Elegance Choker Necklace [page 21] is the only project woven with two.) Two-needle RAW is sometimes referred to as cross-weaving because at some point, you cross two needles through the same bead. Figure 8 shows how the first unit is made with two needles. Figure 9 shows how more units are added to make a row.

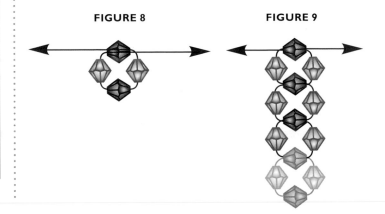

FIGURE 8   FIGURE 9

FIGURE 10

FIGURE 11

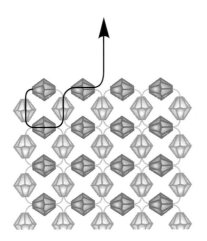

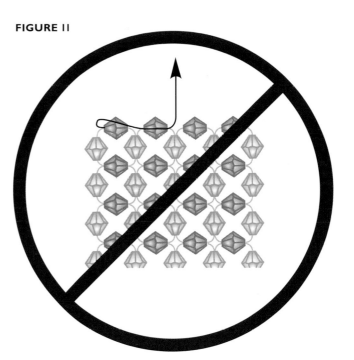

The advantage of beading with one needle is that you have better control of your tension. Tension refers to how tightly or loosely your beads are woven together. While tension is tighter with one needle, two-needle weaving allows the beadwork to stay soft and supple. Also, it's a quicker way to get to a certain point, rather than meandering through several beads to get where you need to be. Two-needle RAW requires fewer passes through the beads, thus reducing the risk of breaking a bead or filling up a bead hole too soon because you have too much thread going through it.

ADDING NEW THREAD

Stop weaving when you have only 6 inches (15.2 cm) of thread left to stitch with. Cut a new piece of thread in a length that you are comfortable with. Thread this new thread onto a needle and add a stop bead. Pass the needle through the bead out of which the old thread is exiting, in the same direction as the old thread. Continue to weave with the new thread.

FINISHING THREADS

After you're finished with all the beading, you need to weave in your loose threads. Remove any stop beads. Work with one thread at a time. Add a needle onto one thread, and weave it through some beads in the beadwork, retracing your established thread paths. Figure 10 shows a small swatch of beadwork and the right way (as well as the wrong way, as in figure 11) to weave. Once that's done, tie a half-hitch knot. Then pass

through a few more beads and trim away the excess thread using scissors or a thread burner.

Tying a Half-Hitch Knot

You should place the knot between two beads. Pass the needle underneath the thread where you want the knot to be. Pull the thread until you have a loop. Pass the needle through the loop. Slowly pull the thread so that the loop doesn't catch on anything and shrinks into a knot between the two beads (figure 12).

FIGURE 12

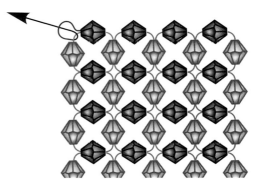

sassy stripes tennis bracelet

This bracelet has a double row of crystals woven in one-needle RAW stitch. From a very young age, I was drawn to stripes. Big, bold bands and skinny pinstripes— my favorite items of clothing always featured lines and strips of color. It's no wonder that I dreamed up a bracelet full of striped goodness!

YOU'LL NEED

76 olivine crystal bicones, 4 mm (A)

76 crystal dorado crystal bicones, 4 mm (B)

Size 11° bronze seed beads, 1 g

Single-strand clasp

FireLine, 6-pound test

Scissors

Thread conditioner (optional)

Size 11 or 12 beading needles

Thread burner (optional)

Beading mat

Measuring tape

DIMENSIONS

7¼ inches (18.4 cm) long

DIFFICULTY LEVEL

Easy beginner

1 Cut and condition 2½ yards (2.3 m) of thread. Thread a needle onto one end.

2 For use as a stop bead, select a seed bead that's a different color than the seed beads you're using in the project. (That way, you won't confuse it with the other seed beads.) String it on and slide it so it's 11 inches (27.9 cm) from the far end. Pass through it again to temporarily secure it.

3 String two A crystals and two B crystals. Slide them down to your stop bead.

4 Pass through the first A crystal to form a square. Continue to pass through one A crystal and one B crystal. A square is made.

5 String two A crystals and one B crystal. Pass through the B crystal from the last square. A new square is made.

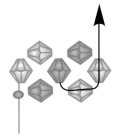

6 Continue to pass through two A crystals.

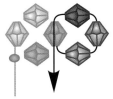

7 String one A crystal and two B crystals. Pass through one A crystal from the last square. A new square is made.

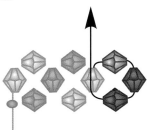

8 Continue to pass through one A crystal and one B crystal.

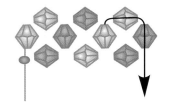

9 Continue to repeat steps 5 to 8 until you've reached the desired length, being sure to end up with an odd amount of squares. Keep in mind that the clasp will add approximately an extra 1 inch (2.5 cm).

10 String two A crystals and one B crystal. Pass through one B crystal from the last square. This is the last square of the first row.

11 Continue to pass through one A crystal.

12 String two B crystals and one A crystal. Pass through one A crystal from the previous square. This is the new square of the second row.

13 Continue to pass through two B crystals and one A crystal.

14 Pass across through one B crystal of the next square from the first row.

15 String one B crystal and one A crystal. Pass vertically through one A crystal from the previous square from the second row and through one B crystal from the square from the first row. One new square is made.

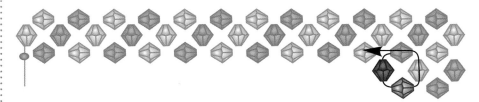

16 Continue to pass through one B crystal in the new square.

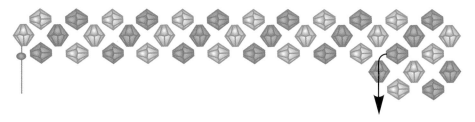

17 String one B crystal and one A crystal. Pass backward through the A crystal of the next square in the first row. Pass vertically through one B crystal of the previous square in the second row. One new square is made.

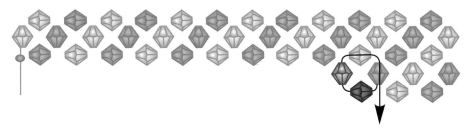

18 Continue to pass through one B crystal and one A crystal in the new square.

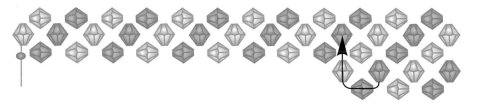

19 Continue to repeat steps 14 to 18 until you've reached the end of your bracelet. Pass the remaining thread through a few beads. Use this opportunity to tighten up any loose areas by passing through the crystals in the square again. When you're done, weave to a place where you want to tie a knot. Finish off the thread.

20 Slide off the stop bead. Thread a needle onto the tail end.

21 String one seed bead. Pass through one B crystal. String five seed beads and one clasp end.

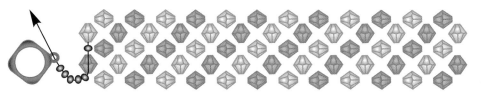

22 Pass back down through one seed bead. String four seed beads and pass across through one A crystal, one seed bead, and one B crystal to form a triangle. Pass through all of the beads and the clasp end in the triangle to reinforce the clasp.

23 Pass through a few beads. Finish off the thread.

24 Cut and condition 11 inches (27.9 cm) of thread. Thread a needle onto one end. Attach a stop bead and position it 6 inches (15.2 cm) from the far end. (If you need to jog your memory, step 2 explains how to attach a stop bead.)

25 Pass the needle through the last A crystal, weaving toward the middle of your bracelet. Repeat steps 21 to 23 to attach the other clasp end.

26 Slide off the stop bead and finish off the thread.

Try it on! Doesn't it look great?

pearly elegance choker

Every woman needs a statement piece, and this short necklace is it. This classic beauty can be worn with either casual or formal attire. It includes crystals, seed beads, and pearls and is woven using two-needle RAW. Make a short version to wear around your wrist.

YOU'LL NEED

47 crystal golden shadow crystal bicones, 6 mm

92 powder almond glass pearls, 6 mm

Size 8° light mauve seed beads, 2 g

Toggle clasp, ¾ to 1 inch (1.9 to 2.5 cm) long

FireLine, 8-pound test

Scissors

Thread conditioner (optional)

2 size 10 or 12 beading needles

Plastic thread bobbin

Thread burner (optional)

Beading mat

Measuring tape

DIMENSIONS

16 inches (40.6 cm) long

DIFFICULTY LEVEL

Easy beginner

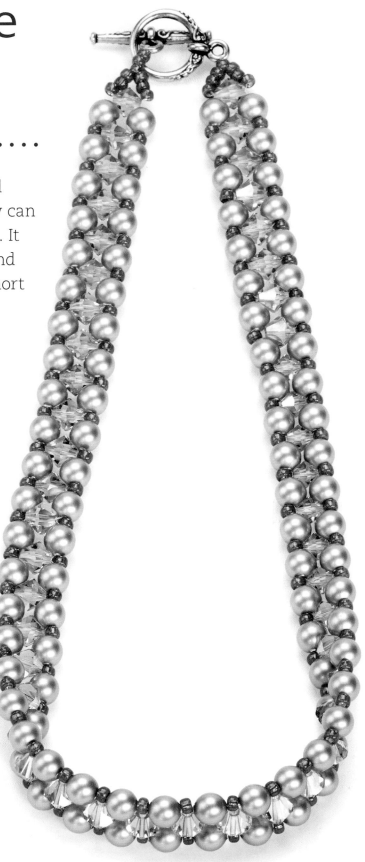

1 Cut and condition approximately 1½ yards (1.4 m) of thread. Thread one needle onto each end. Using one of the needles, string on one bicone and center it on the thread.

2 On each needle, string one glass pearl. With one needle, string one bicone. Pass the other needle through the bicone horizontally so that one needle exits out of the left side and the other needle exits out of the right side of the bead. You now have a square. Slide this first square down to the center of the thread.

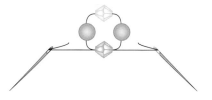

3 Continue to repeat step 2 until both threads are approximately 6 inches (15.2 cm) long.

4 On each needle, string three seed beads. Hold both needles together and string on one seed bead and one clasp end.

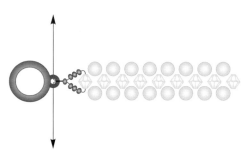

5 Pass both needles back down through one seed bead.

With one needle, pass through a few beads. Finish off the thread. Finish off the other thread.

6 Cut and condition 2 yards (1.8 m) of thread. Thread one needle onto each end again. With one needle, pass through the bicone at the end of your strip.

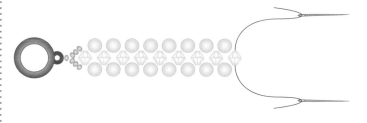

7 Continue to repeat step 2 until you're ¼ inch (6 mm) short of reaching your desired length. (You do this because your piece will shrink approximately ¾ inch [1.9 cm], while your clasp ending will add an extra 1 inch [2.5 cm]. Taking both of these amounts into account, the end result is a net extra ¼ inch [6 mm] added to the piece.)

8 Repeat steps 4 and 5 to add the other clasp end and to finish off the thread.

9 Cut and condition 1½ yards (1.4 m) of thread. Wrap half of the thread onto a thread bobbin. Thread a needle onto the other end.

10 At one end, pass through one pearl, one bicone, and one pearl to reach the other side.

11 String one seed bead. Pass through the next pearl. Repeat this all the way down one side of your piece.

After exiting out of the last pearl, pass through a few more beads. Finish off the thread.

12 Unwind the thread from the bobbin. Thread a needle onto this end. Repeat step 11 to complete the other side.

Go try on the necklace and admire yourself in the mirror!

sweet lattice bracelet

Lovely as lace, this delicate pattern shows that RAW isn't just for making squares. Weave pretty little diamonds to form this net-like beaded fabric.

YOU'LL NEED

Size 11° metallic peach cylinder beads, 8 g (A)

Size 11° matte transparent peach seed beads, 4 g (B)

2 padparadscha pink round crystals, 8 mm

FireLine, 6-pound test

Scissors

Thread conditioner (optional)

Size 11 or 12 beading needles

Plastic thread bobbin

Thread burner (optional)

Beading mat

Measuring tape

DIMENSIONS

7¾ inches (19.7 cm) long

DIFFICULTY LEVEL

Experienced beginner

1 Cut and condition 5½ yards (5 m) of thread. Wrap 3 yards (2.7 m) onto the bobbin. Thread a needle onto the other end. String one A and slide it next to the bobbin.

2 String one B, one A, one B, one A, one B, one A, and one B. Pass through the first A to form a diamond. Position your first diamond up against the bobbin.

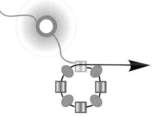

3 Pass through one B and one A.

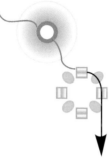

4 String one B, one A, one B, one A, one B, one A, and one B. Pass through the A from the last diamond to form a new diamond.

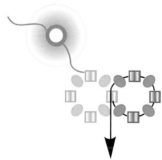

5 Pass through one B, one A, one B, and one A of the new diamond.

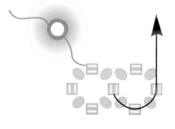

6 String one B, one A, one B, one A, one B, one A, and one B. Pass through the A from the last diamond to form a new diamond.

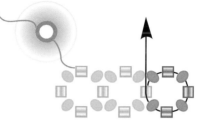

7 Pass through one B, one A, one B, and one A of the new diamond.

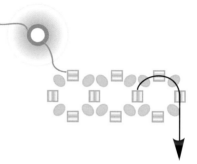

8 Repeat steps 4 to 7. This will complete the first row. You should have a total of five diamonds.

9 Pass through one B and one A of the last diamond.

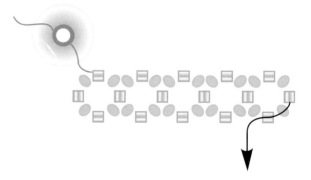

10 String one B, one A, one B, one A, one B, one A, and one B. Pass through the A from the last diamond to form a new diamond. This is the first diamond of the new row.

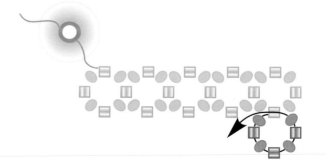

11 Pass through one B and one A.

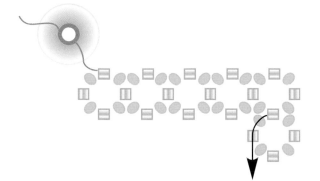

12 String one B, one A, one B, one A, and one B. Pass backward through the A of the next diamond of the previous row.

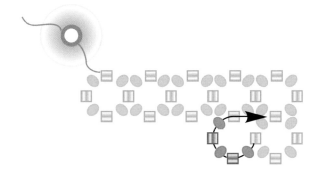

13 String one B. Pass through the A of the last diamond to create a new diamond. Pass through one B, one A, one B, and one A of the new diamond.

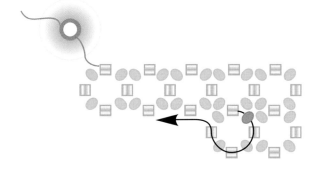

14 String one B. Pass through the A of the next diamond of the previous row.

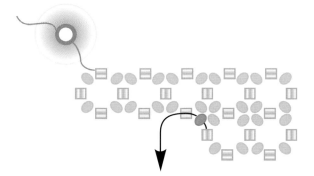

15 String one B, one A, one B, one A, and one B. Pass through the A of the last diamond to form a new diamond.

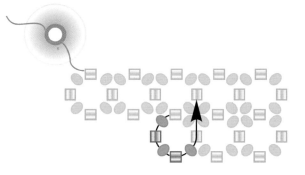

16 Pass through one B, one A, one B, and one A of the new diamond.

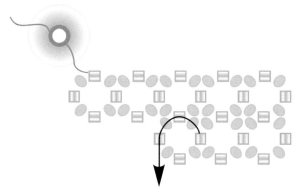

17 Repeat steps 12 to 16 to complete the new row.

18 Pass through one B and one A of the last diamond. Flip your beadwork.

19 Continue to repeat steps 10 to 18 until you have about 11 inches (27.9 cm) of thread remaining. Be sure to exit out of an A at the edge of a completed row. You do not have to flip your beadwork to move on to the next step.

20 String two Bs and pass through the next A. String four Bs, one 8-mm bead, and three Bs. Pass back down through the 8-mm bead and one B. String three Bs and pass through one A, two Bs, and one A to create a triangle. Pass through all of these beads again to reinforce this attachment.

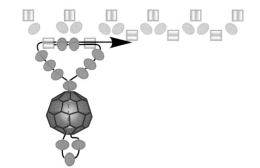

21 Pass through one B, one A, one B, one A, one B, one A, one B, and one A.

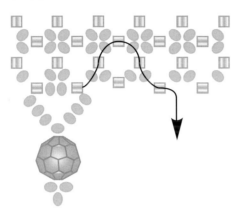

22 Repeat step 20 to attach the other bead clasp, then pass through a few more beads. Finish off the thread. You're halfway finished.

23 Unwind the thread from the bobbin. Thread a needle onto this end. Weave your way to come out the other side by passing through one B, one A, one B, one A, one B, one A, one B, one A, one B, one A, one B, one A, one B, one A, one B, one A, one B, one A, one B, one A, one B, and one A.

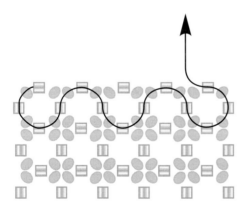

24 Repeat steps 10 to 18 until you've reached your desired length. Don't forget that the beaded clasp ends will add approximately 1 inch (2.5 cm) to the total beaded bracelet. Be sure to exit out of an A at the edge of a completed row.

25 String two Bs. Pass through the next A.

26 String seven Bs. Pass through one A, two Bs, and one A to form a half circle.

27 Pass through four Bs in that half circle to come out of the "peak bead."

28 String one A, one B, one A, one B, one A, one B, one A, one B, one A, one B, one A, one B, one A, one B, one A, one B, and one A. Pass

through the peak bead to form a circle. Continue to pass through all of the beads in the circle two more times. Make sure you're exiting the peak bead when you're done. This will reinforce the circle.

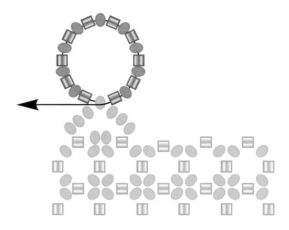

29 Pass through three Bs, one A, two Bs, one A, one B, one A, one B, one A, one B, one A, one B, and one A.

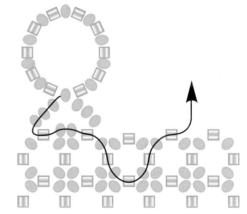

30 Repeat steps 25 to 28 to add the other circle. Pass through a few beads. Finish off the thread.

TIP: Before wearing the bracelet, test that the beaded clasp works. Pass the 8-mm beads through their proper circle loops a few times to make sure each passes through them. The key to these types of closures is for the loop to be loose enough for a large bead or button to go through it but not so loose that the bead slips out during wear.

Over time, the loop will loosen and may have to be tightened. To do this, simply weave in a new piece of thread and pass through the beads in the circle again to tighten it. As with any sort of beaded finery, these pieces must be handled with care.

Put on your bracelet, and enjoy the compliments!

seeds 'n' lace bracelet

Thinking back to lazy summer afternoons growing up, I remember my neighbor's flower garden. She had a wooden trellis up against the side of the house with the most beautiful blooms all over it. That inspired this lacy, floral band, which uses one needle.

YOU'LL NEED

Size 8° metallic mauve seed beads, 5 g (A)

Size 15° magenta seed beads, 1 g (B)

Size 15° gold seed beads, 4 g (C)

Size 11° lime seed beads, 2 g (D)

3 light amethyst AB round crystals, 6 mm

FireLine, 6-pound test

Scissors

Thread conditioner (optional)

Size 11 or 12 beading needles

Plastic thread bobbin

Thread burner (optional)

Beading mat

Measuring tape

DIMENSIONS

7½ inches (19 cm) long

DIFFICULTY LEVEL

Advanced

1 Cut and condition 6 yards (5.5 m) of thread. Wrap 3 yards (2.7 m) onto the bobbin. Thread a needle onto the other end. String one A and slide it down to the bobbin.

2 String three As. Pass through the A next to the bobbin to form a clover.

3 String one B. Pass through the next A. Repeat this three more times, going around the clover. One flower is made.

4 Pass through one B and one A.

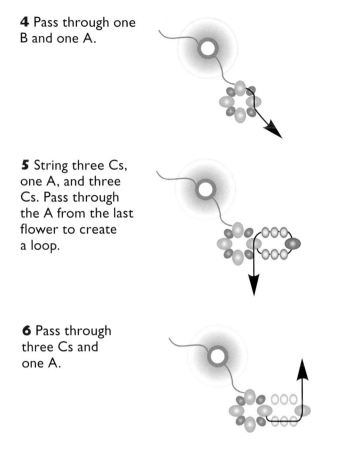

5 String three Cs, one A, and three Cs. Pass through the A from the last flower to create a loop.

6 Pass through three Cs and one A.

7 String three As. Pass through the A that your thread is exiting out of, from the last loop, to form a new clover.

8 String one B. Pass through the next A. Repeat this three more times, going around your new clover. A new flower is made.

9 Pass through one B, one A, one B, and one A.

10 Repeat steps 5 to 8 to make another loop and flower.

11 Pass through one B, one A, one B, one A, one B, and one A. You've completed one flower row.

12 String three Cs, one D, three Cs, one A, three Cs, one D, and three Cs. Pass through the A your thread was exiting to form a loop.

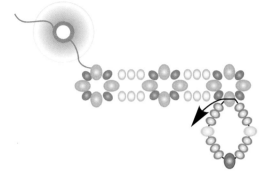

13 Pass through three Cs and one D.

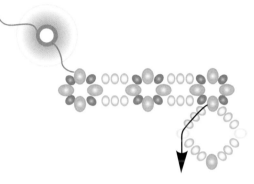

14 String three Cs, one A, three Cs, one D, and three Cs. Pass backward through the top A of the next flower. String three Cs. Pass through the D from the last loop to complete this new loop.

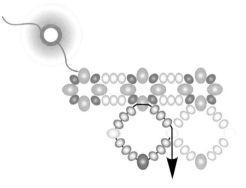

15 In the new loop, pass through three Cs, one A, three Cs, and one D.

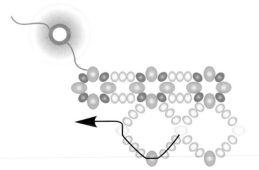

16 String three Cs. Pass through the top A of the next flower. String three Cs, one D, three Cs, one A, and three Cs. Pass through the D from the last loop to complete this new loop.

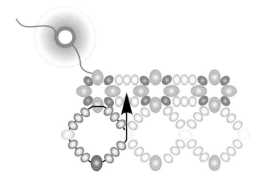

17 In the new loop, pass through three Cs, one A, three Cs, one D, three Cs, and one A. One loop row is done.

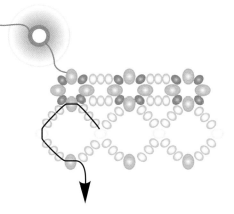

18 Repeat steps 2 to 6 to create a flower and a small loop.

19 Pass through the A of the next loop. String two As. Pass through the A of the last small loop to create a new clover.

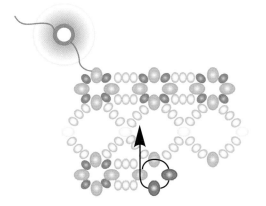

20 Repeat step 3.

21 Pass through one B, one A, one B, and one A.

22 Repeat steps 5 and 6 to create a small loop.

23 Repeat steps 19 and 20 to make a new flower.

24 Pass through one B, one A, one B, one A, one B, and one A. You've completed one flower row.

25 Repeat steps 12 to 17 to create a loop row.

26 Continue to repeat steps 18 to 25, making rows of flowers and loops. End with a row of flowers. Make sure you have about 12 inches (30.5 cm) of thread left to make the clasp.

27 String three Cs, one D, one 6-mm bead, and three Cs. Pass back through the 6-mm bead and one D. String three Cs. Pass through the end A to complete the triangle. Pass through all the beads in the triangle again to reinforce it. Make sure you're exiting from the A.

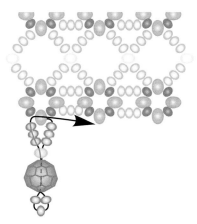

28 Pass through one B, one A, three Cs, one A, one B, and one A.

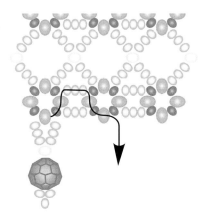

29 Repeat steps 27 and 28 to attach the second 6-mm bead. Repeat step 27 to add the last 6-mm bead, then pass through a few more beads. Finish off the thread.

30 Unwind the thread from the bobbin. Thread a needle onto this end.

31 Pass through one B, one A, one B, one A, one B, one A, three Cs, one A, one B, one A, one B, one A, three Cs, one A, one B, one A, one B, one A, one B, and one A.

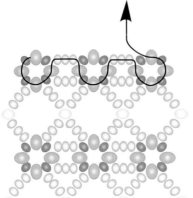

32 Flip the piece so that your beadwork will match the direction of the thread path in the illustrations. Repeat steps 12 to 17 to create a loop row.

33 Continue to repeat steps 18 to 25, making rows of flowers and loops until you've reached your desired length, ending with a row of flowers. Keep in mind that the beaded clasp will add an extra ½ inch (1.3 cm) to your bracelet.

34 String three Cs, one D, and three Cs. Pass through the A you were exiting out of to form a circle.

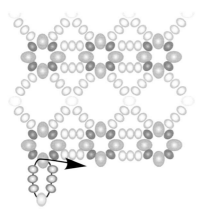

35 Pass through three Cs and one D. The D bead is your "peak bead."

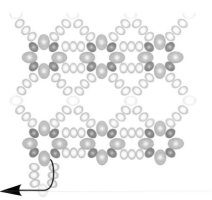

36 String 13 Ds. Pass through the peak bead to form a circle. Pass through all of the Ds in the circle two more times. You should be exiting from a peak bead.

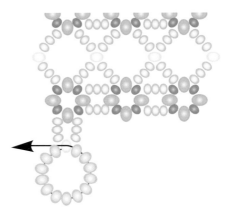

37 Pass through three Cs, one A, one B, one A, three Cs, one A, one B, and one A.

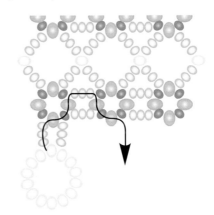

38 Repeat steps 34 to 37 to make the second beaded circle.

39 Repeat steps 34 to 36 to make the last beaded circle. Pass through a few beads. Finish off the thread.

TIP: Before wearing the bracelet, test that the beaded clasp works. Pass the 6-mm beads through their proper circle loops a few times to make sure each passes through them. The key to these types of closures is for the loop to be loose enough for a large bead or button to go through it but not so loose that the bead slips out during wear.

Over time, the loop will loosen and may have to be tightened. To do this, simply weave in a new piece of thread and pass through the beads in the circle again to tighten it. As with any sort of beaded finery, these pieces must be handled with care.

Congratulations! Your bracelet is ready to wear.

3

increasing & decreasing

· · · · · · · · · · · · · · · ·

Think of RAW as a series of blocks stacked together. You can stagger the blocks in one direction to create a diagonal.

FIGURE I **FIGURE 2** **FIGURE 3**

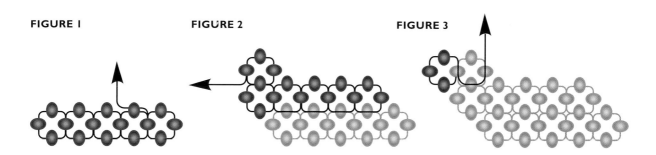

Refer back to Chapter 2 (Basic Flat RAW) to see how to make a row in RAW. Figure 1 illustrates how you start with one row and weave your way to exit out of the second-to-last unit. Figure 2 shows how the second row is added, as well as the first unit of the third row. Figure 3 shows how to increase a row by adding an extra unit. Striped Chic Bracelet (page 32) also illustrates this in detail.

Or you can increase and decrease the blocks to create shapes (figure 4). This can be seen in Hearts Aflutter Earrings (page 40), Jagged Bracelet (page 36), and Amazon Jewels Necklace (page 43).

FIGURE 4

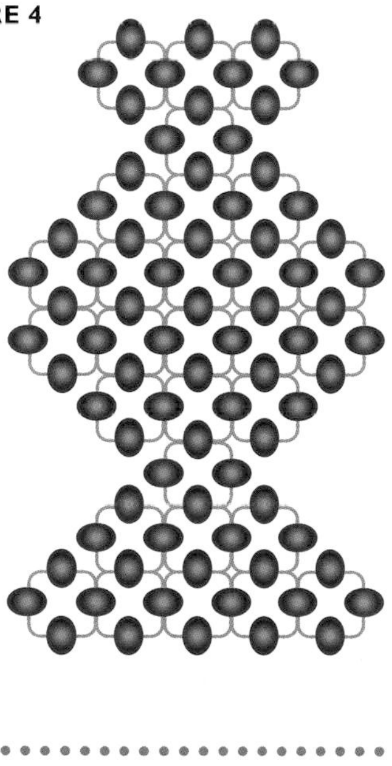

striped chic bracelet

This bracelet is woven with one needle, demonstrating how you can tilt simple squares and turn the usual grid made in RAW into something quite interesting. Crystals in a diagonal row, partnered with skinny beaded lines, add just enough glitz. There is beauty in simplicity.

YOU'LL NEED

140 aquamarine blue crystal bicones, 4 mm (A)

Size 11° gold cylinder beads, 2 g (B)

2 bronze crystal pearls, 6 mm

FireLine, 6-pound test

Scissors

Thread conditioner (optional)

Size 11 or 12 beading needles

Plastic thread bobbin

Thread burner (optional)

Beading mat

Measuring tape

DIMENSIONS

7½ inches (19 cm) long

DIFFICULTY LEVEL

Easy beginner

1 Cut and condition 5 yards (4.6 m) of thread. Wrap half of the thread onto the bobbin. Thread a needle onto the other end. String one A and slide it down to the bobbin.

2 String two Bs, one A, and two Bs. Pass through the first A to form a square.

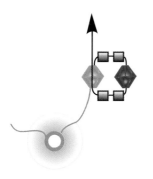

3 Pass through two Bs and one A.

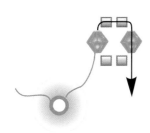

4 String two Bs, one A, and two Bs. Pass through the A you were exiting out of from the last square to form a new square.

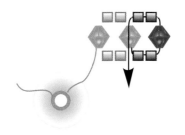

5 In the new square, pass through two Bs and one A.

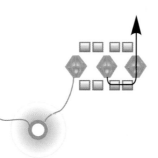

6 Repeat steps 2 to 4 to make the third and fourth squares.

7 In the previous square (not the new square), pass through two Bs, one A, and two Bs. One row is complete.

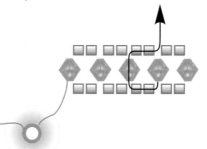

8 String one A, two Bs, and one A. Pass through the two Bs from the square you are exiting out of to form a new square. This is the first square of the new row.

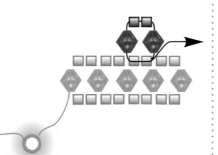

9 In the new square, pass through one A, two Bs, and one A. Continue to pass through the next two Bs in the next square.

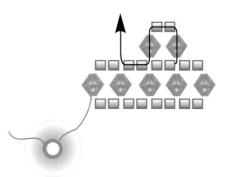

10 String one A and two Bs. Pass through the A from the last square made. A second square is made. Continue to pass through the two Bs in the new square.

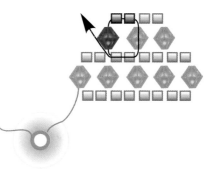

11 Pass through the A of the new square.

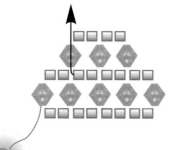

12 String two Bs and one A. Pass through the next two Bs, going backward. Continue to pass through the A from the last square. The third square is made.

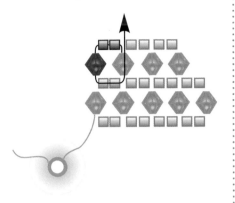

13 In the new square, pass through two Bs and one A.

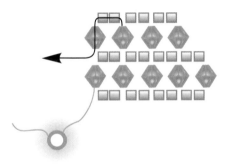

14 String two Bs, one A, and two Bs. Pass through the A from the last square. The fourth square is made. Moving back toward the second square, pass through two Bs, one A, and two Bs. A new row is completed.

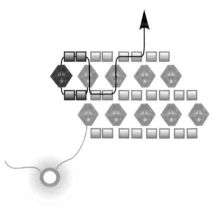

15 Continue to repeat steps 8 to 14, adding new rows. Stop when you have at least 12 inches (30.5 cm) of thread left.

16 Pass through one A, two Bs, one A, and two Bs of the end square.

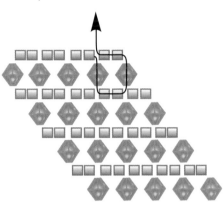

17 String three Bs, one 6-mm bead, and one B. Pass back down through the 6-mm bead and one B. String two Bs and pass across through the two Bs you were exiting out of to form a triangle. Pass through all of the Bs and the 6-mm bead to reinforce this end.

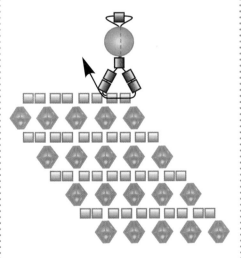

18 Moving toward the last square, pass through one A, two Bs, one A, two Bs, one A, two Bs, one A, and two Bs.

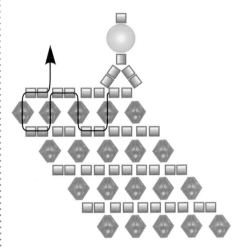

19 Repeat step 17 to add the 6-mm bead to the other end. Pass through a few beads. Finish off the thread. You've completed one end.

20 Unwind the thread from the bobbin. Thread a needle onto this end.

21 Moving toward the next square, pass through two Bs, one A, two Bs, one A, and two Bs.

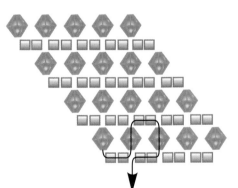

22 Continue to repeat steps 8 to 14 to add new rows until you've reached your desired length. The clasp will add an extra ½ inch (1.3 cm) to your beaded bracelet.

23 Pass through one A, two Bs, one A, and two Bs of the end square.

24 String five Bs. Pass through the same two Bs you were exiting out of to form a half circle.

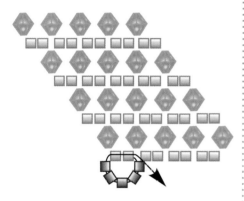

25 Pass through three Bs so that you are exiting out of the "peak bead." String 15 Bs. Pass through the peak bead to create a circle. Pass through all of the Bs in the circle once more to reinforce. Make sure you exit out of the peak bead.

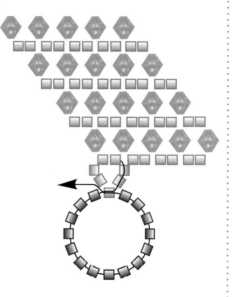

26 Moving toward the end square, pass through four Bs, one A, two Bs, one A, two Bs, one A, two Bs, one A, and two Bs.

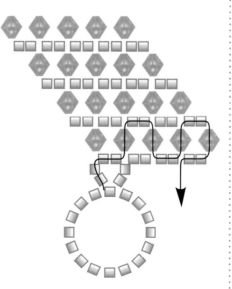

27 Repeat steps 24 and 25 to add the other loop. Pass through a few beads. Finish off the thread.

TIP: Before wearing the bracelet, test that the beaded clasp works. Pass the 6-mm beads through their proper circle loops a few times to make sure each passes through them. The key to these types of closures is for the loop to be loose enough for a large bead or button to go through it but not so loose that the bead slips out during wear.

Over time, the loop will loosen and may have to be tightened. To do this, simply weave in a new piece of thread and pass through the beads in the circle again to tighten it. As with any sort of beaded finery, these pieces must be handled with care.

Do a little victory dance: you're finished!

jagged bracelet

Create a bracelet with edgy appeal. You'll use one needle to increase and decrease in RAW to create the jagged sides. This design can easily be adapted to be as skinny or as wide as you desire.

YOU'LL NEED

Size 11° gold cylinder beads, 2 g (A)

124 emerald green iris fire-polished glass beads, 3 mm (B)

Single-strand clasp

Size D nylon beading thread

Scissors

Thread conditioner (optional)

Size 11 beading needles

Thread burner (optional)

Beading mat

Measuring tape

DIMENSIONS

7½ inches (19 cm) long

DIFFICULTY LEVEL

Easy beginner

1 Cut and condition 2 yards (1.8 m) of thread. Thread a needle onto one end. String one size 11° seed bead. Pass through it again to temporarily secure it. This is the stop bead. Position your stop bead approximately 12 inches (30.5 cm) from the far end. At a later point, this tail thread will be used to attach one clasp end. String one A.

2 String one B, one A, and one B. Pass through the first A and one B to form a rectangle.

3 String one A, one B, and one A. Pass through one B from the last rectangle to form a new rectangle.

4 In the new rectangle, pass through one A and one B.

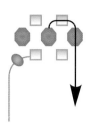

5 String one A, one B, and one A. Pass through one B from the last rectangle to form a new rectangle. This finishes one row.

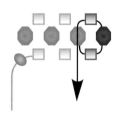

6 In the new rectangle, pass through one A, one B, and one A.

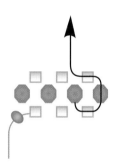

7 String one B, one A, and one B. Pass through one A from the last rectangle to form a new rectangle of a new row.

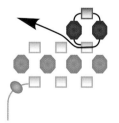

8 In the new rectangle, pass through one B, one A, and one B.

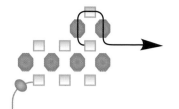

9 String one A, one B, and one A. Pass through one B from the last rectangle to form a new rectangle. In the last rectangle, continue to pass through one A and one B.

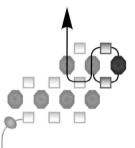

10 String one A and one B. Pass through one A from the last row and one B of the last rectangle to form a new rectangle.

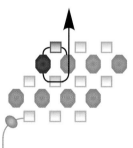

11 In the new rectangle, pass through one A and one B. Continue to pass through one A from the last row.

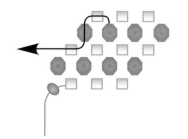

12 String one B and one A. Pass through one B from the last rectangle to form a new rectangle. Continue to pass through one A from the last row.

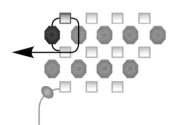

13 In the new rectangle, pass through one B.

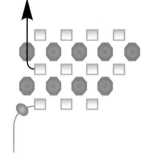

14 String one A, one B, and one A. Pass through one B and one A from the last rectangle to form a new rectangle. This completes your new row.

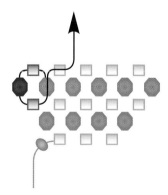

15 String one B, one A, and one B. Pass through the first A and one B to create the first rectangle for a new row. Refer to the illustration in step 2.

16 String one A and one B. Pass through one A from the last row to form a new rectangle. Continue to pass through one B from the last rectangle.

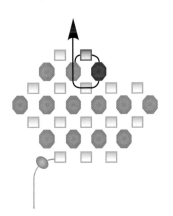

17 In the new rectangle, pass through one A and one B. Pass through one A from the last row.

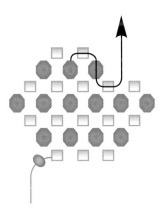

18 String one B and one A. Pass through one B from the last rectangle to form a new rectangle. This is the last rectangle of your new row. Continue to pass through one A from the last row.

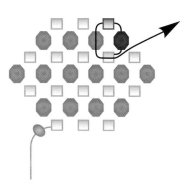

19 In the new rectangle, pass through one B and one A.

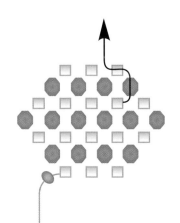

20 String five As. Pass through one A from the last rectangle to form a new rectangle of a new row.

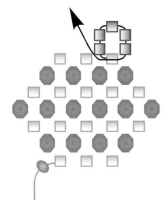

21 In the new rectangle, pass through two As.

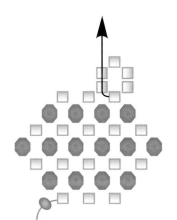

22 String three As. Pass through one A from the last row to form a new rectangle. Pass through two As from the last rectangle.

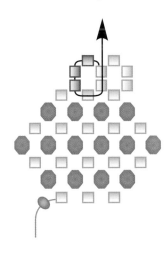

23 In the new rectangle, pass through three As. Pass through one A from the last row.

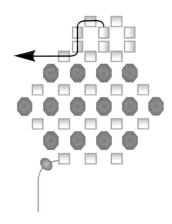

24 String three As. Pass through two As from the last rectangle to form a new rectangle. Pass through one A from the last row. This completes the last rectangle of the new row.

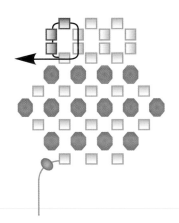

25 In the new rectangle, pass through three As.

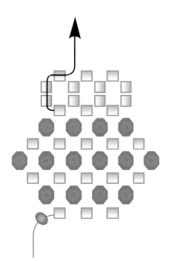

26 Repeat steps 15 to 25 to create one row of Bs and one row of As.

27 Repeat steps 15 to 19 to create one row of Bs.

28 Repeat steps 7 to 19 to create one longer row of Bs and a shorter row of Bs.

29 Repeat steps 20 to 26 to create a bridge of one row of As, one row of Bs, and one row of As.

30 Repeat steps 27 to 28 to create a three-row section of Bs.

31 Continue to repeat steps 20 to 28 until you've reached your desired length. Keep in mind that the ending with the clasp will add approximately 1¼ inches (3.2 cm) to your bracelet. Be sure to end with a three-row section of Bs.

32 String one A. Pass through the next A. Repeat this again.

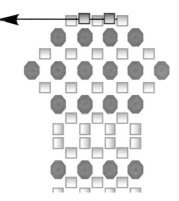

33 String two As, one B, and two As. Pass through five As at the edge of your bracelet.

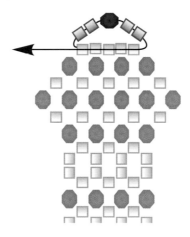

34 Continue to pass through two As and one B.

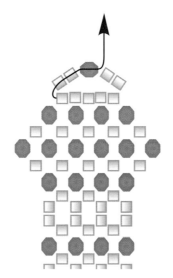

35 String three As and one clasp end. Pass back down through one A. String two As and pass through one B to form a triangle. Pass through all of the As and the clasp end in the triangle once more to reinforce the attachment to the clasp.

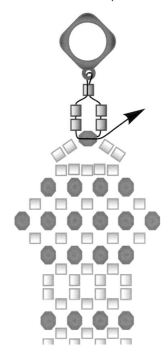

36 Pass through a few beads. Finish off the thread.

37 Remove the stop bead. Thread a needle onto the tail end. Pass through one B, one A, one B, one A, one B, one A, one B, and one A to exit out the other side of your bracelet.

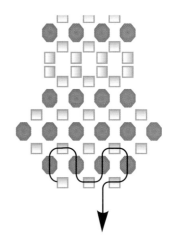

38 Repeat steps 32 to 36 to complete the other end and to finish off your bracelet.

hearts aflutter earrings

Escape from dreary days with these light, sparkly earrings. When I wear them I can't help but shake my head because I love to see these glittery hearts sparkle. Make them in your favorite color. Make several of these hearts and cascade them onto chain for a really long pair of earrings! These hearts are woven with one needle, using a simple increasing and decreasing in right angle weave stitch.

YOU'LL NEED

40 siam crystal bicones, 3 mm (A)

Size 15° silver seed beads, 1 g (B)

2 closed rings, 3 mm

1 pair of earring findings

FireLine, 6-pound test

Scissors

Thread conditioner (optional)

Size 11 or 12 beading needles

Thread burner (optional)

Beading mat

Measuring tape

Chain-nose jewelry pliers

DIMENSIONS

1 inch (2.5 cm) long

DIFFICULTY LEVEL

Experienced beginner

1 Cut and condition 24 inches (61 cm) of thread. String one A.

2 String three As. Pass through the first A to form a square. Position the square about 6 inches (15.2 cm) from the far end of the tail thread. Pass through all four As once more to secure their position on the thread.

3 Pass through two As.

4 String three As. Pass through the A from the last square to form a new square.

5 In the new square, pass through three As.

6 String two As and five Bs. Pass through the A that your thread was exiting out of to form a new square.

7 In the new square, pass through one A.

8 String two As. Pass through two As to form a new square.

9 In the new square, pass through two As.

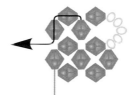

10 String three As. Pass through the A from the last square to form a new square. Continue to pass through three As of the middle square.

11 String three As. Pass through the A from which your thread was exiting to form a new square.

12 In the new square, pass through three As. Continue to pass through one A in the next square.

13 String two As. Pass through two As to form the final square.

14 Pass through all of the As that outline the heart until you're exiting out of the A from which you started. This will reinforce the edges and make your beadwork a little stiffer. Pass through three Bs so that you're coming out of the "peak bead."

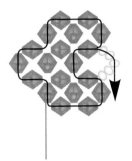

15 String seven Bs. Pass through the peak bead to form an oval. In the oval, pass through four Bs to exit out of the new peak bead.

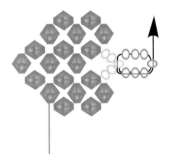

16 String one A, one B, and one closed ring. Pass back down through one B and one A. Pass across through the peak bead. Pass back up through one A, one B, and the closed ring to reinforce it. Pass back down through the two beads and across the peak bead again.

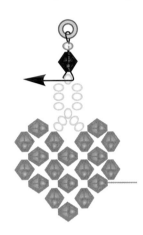

17 Pass through a few beads. Finish off the thread. Thread a needle onto the tail end and finish off the thread.

18 With your chain-nose pliers, twist open the ring end of the earring finding. Link it to the closed ring of the heart charm. Twist the ring closed with your pliers.

19 Repeat steps 1 to 18 to complete your pair of earrings.

Put on your finery, add the earrings, and head out for a romantic evening.

. . . .

variation

. . . .

You can create more elaborate earrings with just a small variation of these instructions.

1 Make four beaded heart shapes as already described (two using white crystals and two using hot pink), then make two larger heart shapes using 4-mm purple bicones.

2 Cut a 2-inch (5.1 cm) piece of chain. Attach a small heart to the fourth link. Attach a large heart at either end of the chain. Attach a small heart midway along the chain between the two that are already attached. Hang the free end of chain to an earring finding.

3 Repeat step 2 to make the second earring.

amazon jewels necklace

Rainforests and exotic plant life come to mind when I think of the Amazon. This design was inspired by the forest's lush green leaves and color palette. Make three-dimensional leaves by increasing and decreasing in right angle weave stitch.

YOU'LL NEED

Size 11° matte teal AB Japanese seed beads, 3 g (A)

Size 11° metallic olive green Japanese seed beads, 7 g (B)

7 light green rondelle beads, 5 x 8 mm (C)

7 amethyst AB crystal bicones, 4 mm (D)

66 bronze round glass beads, 6 mm (E)

2 wire guards/protectors

Single-strand clasp

FireLine, 6-pound test

Scissors

Thread conditioner (optional)

Size 11 beading needles

Thread burner (optional)

Beading mat

Measuring tape

DIMENSIONS

18½ inches (47 cm) long

DIFFICULTY LEVEL

Advanced

Small Leaf

1 Cut and condition 2 yards (1.8 m) of thread. Thread one needle onto one end. String one size 11° seed bead (preferably a different color than the seed beads intended for this project). Pass through it again to temporarily secure it. This is the stop bead. Position it approximately 6 inches (15.2 cm) from the far end.

2 String two As and two Bs. Pass through two As and one B to form the first square or unit for row 1.

3 String two Bs and one A. Pass through one B from the last unit to create the second unit for row 1. Continue to pass through two Bs in the new unit.

4 String one A and two Bs. Pass through one B from the last unit to create the third unit for row 1. Continue to pass through one A and one B in the new unit.

5 String one B and two As. Pass through one B from the last unit to create the fourth unit. Continue to pass through one B in the new unit. This completes row 1.

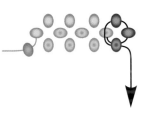

6 String three Bs. Pass through one B from the last unit to create a new unit for row 2. Pass through one B in the new unit.

7 String one B and two As. Pass through one B from the last unit to form a new unit for row 2. In the last unit, pass through two Bs.

8 Pass through the next B from row 1. String two Bs. Pass through one B from the last unit to create the third unit for row 2. Continue to pass through two more Bs in the new unit.

9 String two Bs. Pass through the next B from row 1 to create the fourth unit for row 2. Continue to pass through three Bs in the new unit.

10 Repeat step 8 to create the fifth unit for row 2.

11 String one B and two As. Pass through one B from the last unit to create the sixth unit. Continue to pass through one B in the new unit. This completes row 2.

12 String one A and two Bs. Pass through one B from row 2 to create the first unit of row 3. Continue to pass through one A and two Bs.

13 Pass through the next B from row 2. String two Bs. Pass through one B from the last unit to create the second unit. Continue to pass through two Bs in the new unit.

14 String two Bs. Pass through the next B from row 2 to create the third unit. Continue to pass through three Bs in the new unit.

15 Repeat steps 13 and 14 to create the fourth and fifth units.

16 Pass through the next B from row 2. String one A and one B. Pass through one B from the last unit to create the sixth unit. Continue to pass through one B, one A, and one B in the new unit. This completes row 3.

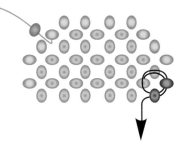

17 String two Bs and one A. Pass through one B from row 3 to create the first unit of row 4. Continue to pass through one B in the new unit.

18 Repeat steps 9 and 10 twice to add four new units to row 4.

19 String one B and one A. Pass through the next B from row 3 to create the sixth unit. Continue to pass through two Bs in the new unit. This completes row 4.

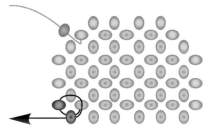

20 String two As and one B. Pass through one B from row 4 to create the first unit of row 5. Continue to pass through two As and one B in the new unit.

21 Repeat steps 13 and 14 twice to create four units for row 5.

22 Pass through the next B from row 4. String two As. Pass through one B from the last unit to create the sixth unit. This completes row 5. In the last row, continue to pass through three Bs.

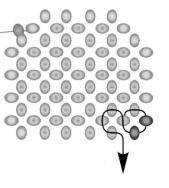

23 String two As and one B. Pass through one B from row 5 to create the first unit of row 6. Continue to pass through two As and one B in the new unit.

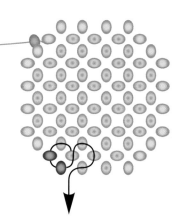

24 Repeat steps 8 and 9 to create the second and third units for row 6.

25 Pass through the next B in row 5. String two As. Pass through one B from the last unit to create the fourth unit. This completes row 6. In the last unit, continue to pass through three Bs.

26 String two As and one B. Pass through one B from row 6 to create the first unit of row 7. Continue to pass through two As and one B in the new unit.

27 Pass through the next B from row 6. String two As. Pass through one B from the last unit to create the second unit. This completes row 7. Continue to pass through one B and two As in the new unit.

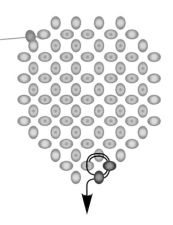

28 String one B and pass through two As to create a point. String one A. Pass through the next 11 As. String one A. Pass through the next 11 As. String one A. Pass through the next two As. Be sure to pull tight enough so that your leaf will curve and puff out.

29 String three As. Skip over one B (the point). Pass through the next 16 As.

30 String two As, one C, and two As. Pass through the three As at the top of the leaf. Continue to pass through two As.

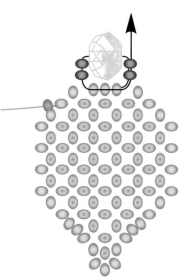

31 String 11 As. Skip over the C and pass through two As and the three As at the top of the leaf to fully outline the C.

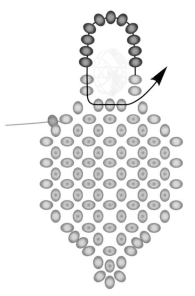

32 Pass through eight As to exit out of the top A.

33 String one B, one D, and three Bs. Pass back down through the D. String one B. Pass through the A you were coming out of.

34 Pass through some beads to tighten up any loose areas or firm up your leaf. Finish off the thread. Remove the stop bead. Thread a needle onto the tail thread and finish off this thread, too. One leaf is done.

35 Repeat steps 1 to 34 to make another small leaf.

Medium Leaf

36 A medium leaf is slightly larger than a small leaf because it has eight rows instead of seven. Repeat steps 1 to 19 to create the first four rows.

37 Repeat steps 12 to 16 to create row 5.

38 String one B and two As. Pass through one B from row 5 to create the first unit of row 6. Continue to pass through one B in the new unit.

39 Repeat steps 9 and 10 twice to add four more units to row 6.

40 String two As. Pass through one B from the previous row to create the sixth unit. This completes row 6. In the last unit, pass through two Bs.

41 String one B and two As. Pass through one B from row 6 to create the first unit of row 7. Continue to pass through one B.

42 String two Bs. Pass through the next B from row 6 to create the second unit. Continue to pass through three Bs in the new unit.

43 Repeat step 13 to create a third unit for row 7.

44 String two As. Pass through one B from the last row to create a fourth unit. This completes row 7. In the last unit, continue to pass through two Bs.

45 String one B and two As. Pass through one B from the last row to create the first unit of row 8. Continue to pass through one B in the new unit.

46 String two As. Pass through one B from the last row to create the second and final unit of row 8. Continue to pass through one B and two As in the new unit.

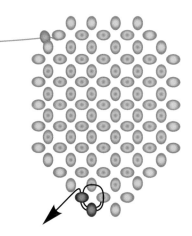

47 String one A. Pass through the next 12 As. String one A. Pass through the next 12 As. String one A. Pass through the next two As. Pull tight so that your beaded leaf puffs out.

48 String one B. Pass through the next 31 As, making your way around the leaf to where you started.

49 String three As. Skip over one B and pass through 17 As.

50 Repeat steps 30 to 34 to attach the beads on top of the leaf. One medium leaf is complete.

51 Repeat steps 36 to 50 to make another medium leaf.

Large Center Leaf

52 A large center leaf is slightly larger than the medium leaf because it has eight units at its widest area and is 11 rows tall. As you make it, follow along with this diagram. Begin by repeating steps 1 to 11 to create two rows.

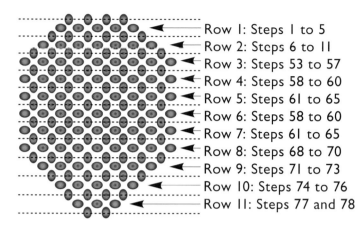

Row 1: Steps 1 to 5
Row 2: Steps 6 to 11
Row 3: Steps 53 to 57
Row 4: Steps 58 to 60
Row 5: Steps 61 to 65
Row 6: Steps 58 to 60
Row 7: Steps 61 to 65
Row 8: Steps 68 to 70
Row 9: Steps 71 to 73
Row 10: Steps 74 to 76
Row 11: Steps 77 and 78

53 String three Bs. Pass through one B from the previous row to create a new unit for row 3. Continue to pass through one B in the new unit.

54 String one B and two As. Pass through one B from the last unit to create a new unit for row 3. In the last unit, continue to pass through two Bs.

55 Repeat steps 13 and 14 twice to add four more units.

56 Repeat step 13 to add a new unit.

57 String one B and two As. Pass through one B from the last unit to create the last unit of row 3. Pass through one B in the new unit.

58 String one A and two Bs. Pass through one B from the previous row to create the first unit of row 4. Pass through one A and two Bs in the new unit.

59 Repeat steps 8 and 9 three times to add six new units.

60 Pass through the next B in the previous row. String one A and one B. Pass through one B from the last unit to create the last unit of row 4. Continue to pass through one B, one A, and one B in the new unit.

61 String two Bs and one A. Pass through one B from the previous row to create the first unit of row 5. Continue to pass through one B in the new unit.

62 Repeat step 14 to create the second unit.

63 Repeat steps 13 and 14 twice to add four units.

64 Repeat step 13 to create the seventh unit.

65 String one B and one A. Pass through one B from the previous row to create the final unit for row 5. Pass through two Bs in the new unit.

66 Repeat steps 58 to 60 to create row 6.

67 Repeat steps 61 to 65 to create row 7.

68 String two As and one B. Pass through one B from the last row to create the first unit of row 8. Pass through two As and one B in the new unit.

69 Repeat steps 8 and 9 three times to create six units.

70 Pass through one B from the last row. String two As. Pass through one B in the last unit to create the final unit of row 8. In the last unit, continue to pass through three Bs.

71 String two As and one B. Pass through one B from the last row to create the first unit of row 9. Continue to pass through two As and one B in the new unit.

72 Repeat steps 13 and 14 twice to create four units.

73 Pass through one B from the last row. String two As. Pass through one B from the last unit to create the final unit for row 9. In the last unit, continue to pass through three Bs.

74 Repeat step 68 to create the first unit of row 10.

75 Repeat steps 8 and 9 to create two units.

76 Repeat step 70 to create the last unit of row 10.

77 String two As and one B. Pass through one B from the last row to create the first unit of row 11. Continue to pass through two As and one B.

78 Pass through one B from the last row. String two As. Pass through one B from the last unit to create the last unit of row 11. Pass through one B and two As in the new unit.

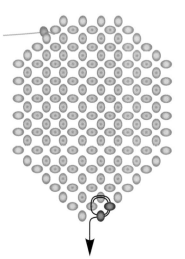

79 String one B. Pass through two As. String one A. Pass through four As. String one A. Pass through 13 As. String one A. Pass through 13 As. String one A. Pass through four As. String one A. Pass through two As. Pull tight enough that your leaf puffs up.

80 String three As. Skip over one B and pass through 23 As.

81 Repeat steps 30 to 34 to attach the beads on top of the leaf. One large leaf is complete.

Assemble the Necklace

82 Cut and condition 1 yard (91.4 cm) of thread. Thread a needle onto one end. Add one stop bead and position it 6 inches (15.2 cm) from the far end.

83 String one D, one B, and one E. Pass through one B, one D, and one B from the small leaf. String one E and one B. Pass through one D to create one square or unit. Continue to pass through one B, one E, one B, one D, and one B.

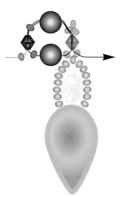

84 String one E. Pass through one B, one D, and one B from the medium leaf. String one E. Pass through one B, one D, and one B from the small leaf. A new square is made. Continue to pass through one E, one B, one D, and one B.

85 String one E. Pass through one B, one D, and one B from the large leaf. String one E. Pass through one B, one D, and one B from the medium leaf. A new square is made. Continue to pass through one E, one B, one D, and one B.

86 String one E. Pass through one B, one D, and one B from the medium leaf. String one E. Pass through one B, one D, and one B from the large leaf. A new square is made. Continue to pass through one E, one B, one D, and one B.

87 String one E. Pass through one B, one D, and one B from the small leaf. String one E. Pass through one B, one D, and one B from the medium leaf. A new square is made. Continue to pass through one E, one B, one D, and one B.

88 String one E, one B, one D, one B, and one E. Pass through one B, one D, and one B from the small leaf.

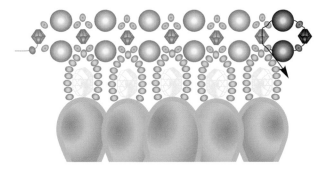

89 Pass through a few beads. Finish off the thread. Remove the stop bead. Thread a needle onto the tail end. Finish off the thread. The centerpiece is complete.

90 Cut and condition 2½ yards (2.3 m) of thread. Thread a needle and position the needle in the middle of the thread. You will be working with doubled thread. String one stop bead. Slide it down to 6 inches (15.2 cm) from the far end.

91 String one E, one B, one wire guard, one clasp end, and one B. Pass back down through one E.

92 String one B and one E. Repeat this pattern until you have a total of 27 Es strung.

93 String one B, one C, and one B. Pass through one E at the end of the centerpiece.

94 String two Bs. Pass through one E. Make sure the two Bs added are placed behind the three Bs that are already there. Repeat this until you're exiting out of the last E of the centerpiece.

95 String one B and one C.

96 String one B and one E. Repeat this until you've got a total of 27 Es strung for this side.

97 String one B, one wire guard, one clasp end, and one B. Pass through one E.

98 Continue to pass through a few beads and tie a half-hitch knot. Repeat this a few more times down your necklace. After tying your final knot, finish off the thread. Remove the stop bead. Thread a needle onto one thread and finish it off. Thread a needle onto the other thread and finish off this thread, too.

Give yourself a pat on the shoulder because your necklace is finished!

4

embellishing

Embellishing can transform an ordinary set of units into something lush and decadent. It's one of the most enjoyable parts of a RAW project.

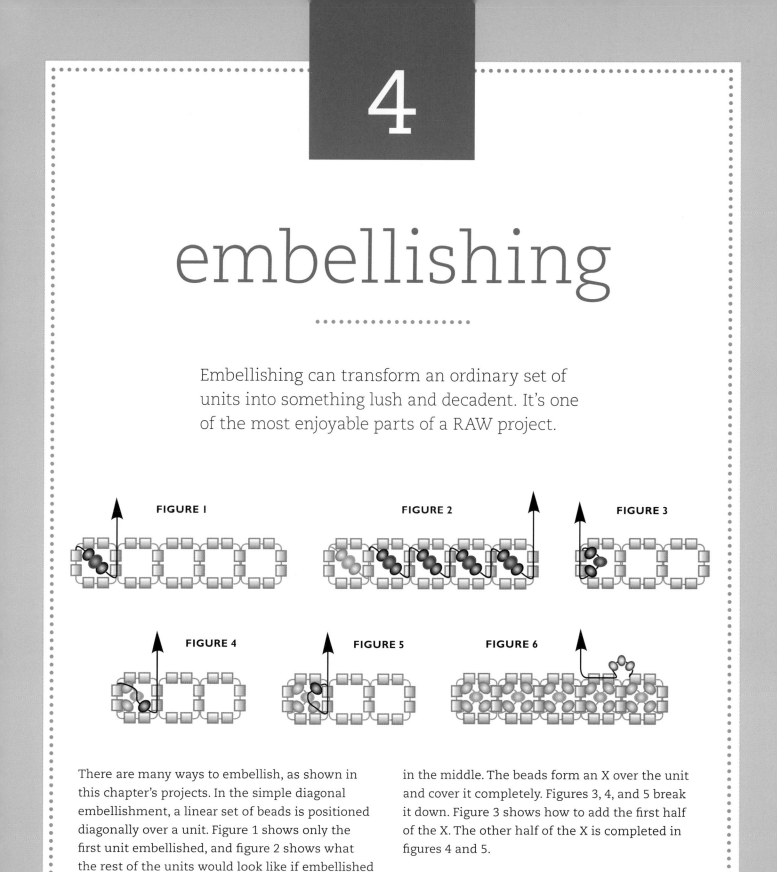

FIGURE 1 **FIGURE 2** **FIGURE 3**

FIGURE 4 **FIGURE 5** **FIGURE 6**

There are many ways to embellish, as shown in this chapter's projects. In the simple diagonal embellishment, a linear set of beads is positioned diagonally over a unit. Figure 1 shows only the first unit embellished, and figure 2 shows what the rest of the units would look like if embellished the same way.

Then there's the X embellishment, where two linear sets of beads cross each other and intersect

in the middle. The beads form an X over the unit and cover it completely. Figures 3, 4, and 5 break it down. Figure 3 shows how to add the first half of the X. The other half of the X is completed in figures 4 and 5.

The simplest way to embellish is to fill a gap with a bead or several beads (figure 6). I like to use this type of embellishing to hide gaps of visible thread, add lacy edging, or expand the beaded piece.

jeweled clover earrings

Femininity and grace radiate from this pair of earrings. Made of round beads, seed beads, and crystals, these earrings involve weaving a simple base and learning how to embellish over and around it.

YOU'LL NEED

8 pale green glass pearls, 6 mm (A)

Size 11° metallic pale green Japanese seed beads, 1 g (B)

2 jet AB crystal bicones, 4 mm (C)

2 closed jump rings, 3 mm

1 pair of lever-back earring findings

FireLine, 6-pound test

Scissors

Thread conditioner (optional)

Size 11 beading needles

Thread burner (optional)

Beading mat

Measuring tape

Chain-nose jewelry pliers

DIMENSIONS

1½ inches (3.8 cm)

DIFFICULTY LEVEL

Experienced beginner

1 Cut and condition 33 inches (83.8 cm) of thread. Thread one needle onto one end. String one A.

2 String one B, one A, one B, one A, one B, one A, and one B. Pass through the first A to form a square or clover. Position your clover 11 inches (27.9 cm) from the end of the thread. This tail thread will be used later to embellish the center of your clover. Pass through all the beads once more. You should be exiting out of the A with the tail thread coming out of it. Pass through one B.

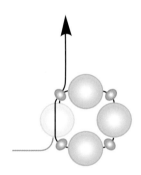

3 String seven Bs. Skip over one A and pass through the next B. Repeat this three more times.

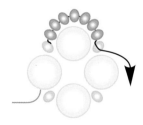

4 Pass through four Bs so that you exit from the seed bead on top of an A.

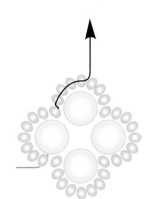

5 String three Bs and one jump ring.

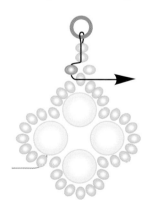

6 Pass back down two Bs. String one B. Pass through the B at the top of the A, which you originally came out of to form a pointed triangle.

Pass once more through all of the Bs and the ring to reinforce the attachment of the ring.

7 Pass through a few beads and tighten up any loose areas. Finish off the thread.

8 Thread a needle onto the tail thread.

9 String three Bs, one C, and three Bs. Pass through the same A you were originally coming out of.

10 Pass through three Bs and the C.

11 String three Bs. Pass through the A directly across from where you were coming out of.

12 String three Bs. Pass through the C. This completes the X embellishment over the center of your clover.

13 Repeat step 7 to finish off your thread. To link your clover to your earring finding, grasp the side of the little link of your earring finding with your pliers. Twist in one direction to open it. Link it to the ring of your clover. Again use your pliers to twist the link closed.

14 Repeat steps 1 to 13 to make the other half and complete your stylish earrings.

Put them on and you're ready to dazzle the world!

Back

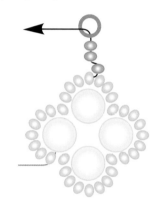

elegance earrings

Romance and femininity swirl about these vintage-inspired earrings. Using one-needle right angle weave stitch, you will weave a beaded cone from crystals and seed beads. A sparkly bead on the end completes this elegant project.

YOU'LL NEED

Size 11° matte olive green seed beads,
  1 g (A)

8 indicolite crystal bicones, 4 mm (B)

Size 15° gold seed beads, 1 g (C)

8 chrysolite opal crystal bicones,
  3 mm (D)

2 pale aqua rondelles, 7 x 11 mm (E)

2 sand opal AB crystal beads, 3 mm (F)

2 gold round beads, 2 mm (optional)

2 gold spacer beads (optional)

2 head pins, 2 inches (5.1 cm)

1 pair of lever-back earring findings

FireLine, 6-pound test

Scissors

Thread conditioner (optional)

Size 12 or 13 beading needles

Thread burner (optional)

Beading mat

Measuring tape

Chain-nose jewelry pliers

Round-nose jewelry pliers

Flush cutters

DIMENSIONS

1½ inches (3.8 cm)

DIFFICULTY LEVEL

Experienced beginner

1 Cut and condition 33 inches (83.8 cm) of thread. Thread a needle onto one end. String one A bead.

2 String three As and pass through the first A to form a clover. Slide the clover down to 8 inches (20.3 cm) from the far end. Pass through all four As in the clover until you are exiting out of the same A with the tail thread exiting from it.

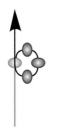

3 String one B, one C, one D, one C, and one B. Pass through the A your thread was exiting out of to form your first triangle. Pass through the next A in the clover.

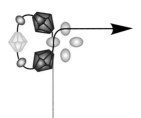

4 String one B, one C, one D, and one C. Pass through the B from the last triangle and the A that you were exiting out of to form your second triangle. Pass through the next A in the clover.

5 Repeat step 4 to create your third triangle. You should be exiting out of the last A in the clover.

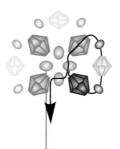

6 Pass through the B from the first triangle.

7 String one C, one D, and one C. Pass through the B from the third triangle to form your fourth triangle. Continue to pass through one A and one B in your new triangle. When you pull tight, your beadwork should pop up. Do not pinch it flat between your fingers.

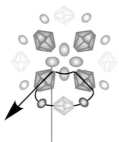

8 In the new triangle, pass through one C, one D, and one C. Continue to pass through the next C.

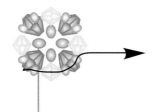

9 String five Cs. Skip over one D and pass through the next two Cs.

10 Repeat step 9 three times, outlining the remaining Ds. Pass through the next four Cs.

11 String one C, one A, and one C. Skip over four Cs and pass through the next three Cs.

> **TIP:** Turn your cone upside down so you can see the Cs more easily.

12 Repeat step 11 three times, going all the way around your beaded cone.

13 Pass through a few beads, then finish off the thread. Thread a needle onto the tail thread.

14 String one C and pass through the next A. Repeat this three more times, inserting a total of four Cs.

15 Pass through a few beads. Finish off the thread. One beaded cone is finished.

16 Stack the following onto one head pin: one A (or one 2-mm round bead), one spacer bead (optional), one E, one beaded cone, and one F.

17 To start this, grab the wire right above the top bead with your chain-nose pliers. With the index finger of your other hand, fold the wire up and over the top of the pliers to make a 90° angle.

18 At the corner, grab the wire with your round-nose pliers. With your other hand, fold the wire up and over the top of the round-nose pliers to begin forming your loop. Reposition your pliers and then continue to fold the wire until it crosses the wire beneath it. This will form a round loop.

19 Hold the round loop with your chain-nose pliers in one hand, and use the other hand to grasp the piece of wire with another pair of pliers. Wrap this wire down to the top of the F bead, creating a short coil. Trim away any excess wire with your flush cutters. Pinch any sharp end into the coil with your chain-nose pliers.

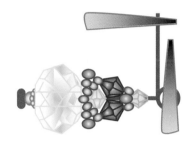

20 Link your wire-wrapped piece onto your earring finding. One earring down, one to go. Repeat all the steps to make the second earring.

RAW channels bracelet

I pore over the priceless diamond bracelets adorning models and movie stars in my favorite fashion magazines, fascinated by the channels of diamonds and their endless sparkle. RAW is the perfect stitch to recreate such designs. Smaller crystals in the center give the bracelet its own everlasting shimmer.

YOU'LL NEED

Size 15° nickel Japanese seed beads, 3 g (A)

Size 11° matte navy blue Japanese seed beads, 5 g (B)

74 Montana crystal bicones, 4 mm (C)

148 sapphire AB crystal bicones, 3 mm (D)

74 blue glass pearls, 4 mm (E)

Two-strand clasp

FireLine, 6-pound test

Scissors

Thread conditioner (optional)

2 size 12 or 13 beading needles

Plastic thread bobbin

Thread burner (optional)

Beading mat

Measuring tape

DIMENSIONS

8 inches (20.3 cm) long

DIFFICULTY LEVEL

Advanced

1 Cut and condition 4 yards (3.7 m) of thread. Wrap 2 yards (1.8 m) onto the bobbin. Thread a needle onto the other end. String one A, one B, and one A. Slide them down to the bobbin.

2 String one A, one B, two As, one B, one A, and one C. Pass through one A, one B, and one A to form a square. Pass through one A, one B, and one A.

3 String one A, two Bs, two As, one B, two As, two Bs, and one A. Pass through one A, one B, and one A from the last square to form a new square. In the new square, pass through one A, two Bs, two As, one B, and one A.

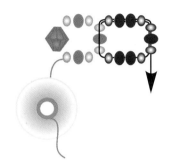

4 String one A, one B, one A, one C, one A, one B, and one A. Pass through one A, one B, and one A from the last square to form a new square. This completes one row. In the new square, pass through one A, one B, one A, one C, one A, one B, and one A.

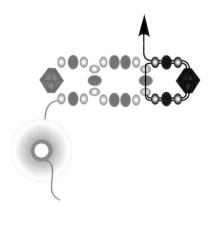

5 String one A, one B, two As, one B, one A, and one C. Pass through one A, one B, and one A from the last square to form a new square of the new row. In the new square, pass through one A, one B, and one A.

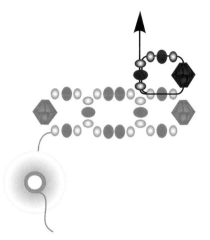

6 String one A, two Bs, two As, one B, and one A. Pass through one A, two Bs, and one A of the square from the last row to form a new square. Pass through one A, one B, and one A from the last square of the new row.

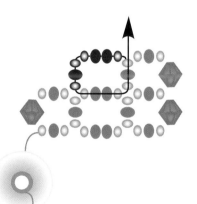

7 In the new square, pass through one A, two Bs, two As, one B, and one A. Continue to pass through one A, one B, and one A.

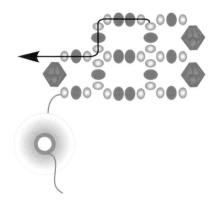

8 String one C, one A, one B, and one A. Pass through one A, one B, and one A from the last square of the new row. Continue to pass through one A, one B, and one A in the square of the last row. This creates a new square and completes your new row.

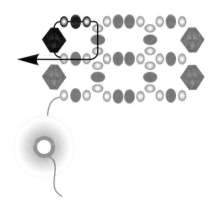

9 In the new square, pass through one C, one A, one B, and one A.

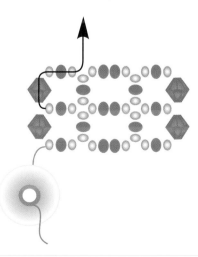

10 Continue to make more rows by repeating steps 4 to 9. Stop when you've completed a row and have a minimum of 6 inches (15.2 cm) of thread left.

11 Pass through a few beads, then finish off the thread.

12 Unwind the thread from your bobbin. Condition it If necessary. Thread a needle onto this end.

13 Pass through one C, one A, one B, two As, one B, two As, two Bs, two As, one B, two As, one B, one A, one C, one A, one B, and one A. This positions your thread so that you can continue to repeat steps 4 to 9 until you've reached your desired length. Keep in mind that the clasp ending will add an extra ¾ inch (1.9 cm) to the total length.

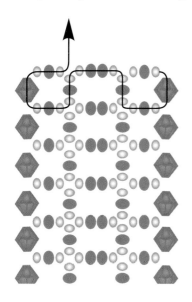

14 Repeat step 11 to finish off the remaining thread.

15 Cut and condition 2 yards (1.8 m) of thread. Thread one needle onto each end. Pass one needle through one A, two Bs, and one A on one end.

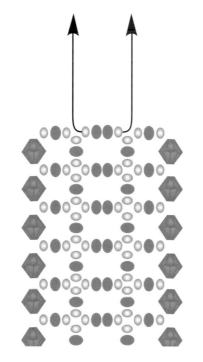

16 On each needle, string one D. With one needle, string one B. Pass the other needle through one B so that one needle exits from the left side and the other needle exits the right side. This forms a triangle.

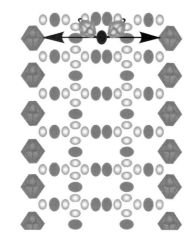

17 On each needle, string one D. With one needle, pass through one A, two Bs, and one A. Pass the other needle through one A, two Bs, and one A so that one needle exits the left side and the other needle exits the right. This completes the X-shaped embellishment over the first square.

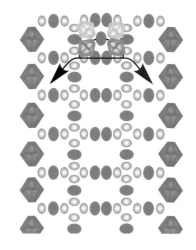

18 Repeat steps 16 and 17 for the entire middle section of your bracelet.

19 With one needle, string 8 As and one clasp loop. Pass through one A, two Bs, and one A. With the same needle, string 8 As and the other clasp loop. Pass through one A, two Bs, and one A. Again with the same needle, pass through the beads, attaching the clasp once more to reinforce it.

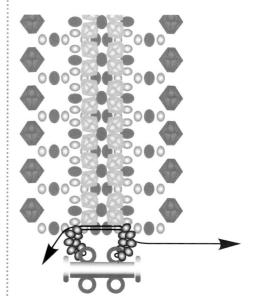

20 With one needle, pass through a few beads. Finish off the thread. Repeat with the other needle to finish off all the threads.

21 Cut and condition 3 yards (2.7 m) of thread. Wrap 1 yard (91.4 cm) onto your bobbin. Thread a needle onto the other end. Pass through one A, one B, and one A on the side with the clasp attached.

22 String one A, one E, and one A. Lay the strung beads diagonally over the square. Pass through one A, one B, and one A. Repeat this all the way down the bracelet.

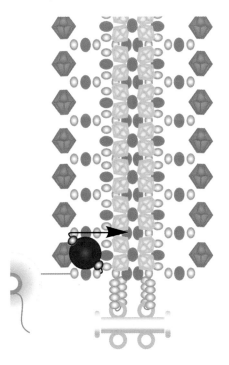

23 Pass through one A, one B, two As, two Bs, two As, one B, two As, two Bs, and one A.

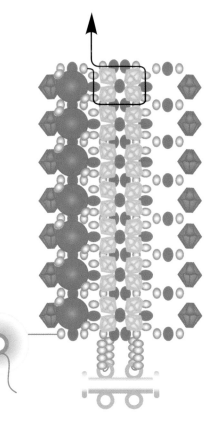

24 Repeat step 19 to attach the clasp to this end.

TIP: If you want the thread path to look exactly like the illustration, flip your bracelet to the back.

25 To position your needle to add pearls to the other side, pass through one A, one B, two As, two Bs, two As, one B, two As, one B, and one A.

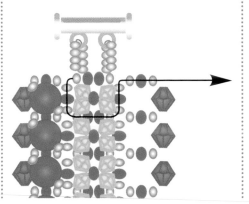

26 String one A, one E, and one A. Lay the strung beads diagonally over the square. Pass through one A, one B, and one A. Repeat this all the way down the bracelet. The embellishments on this side will mirror the ones you made previously.

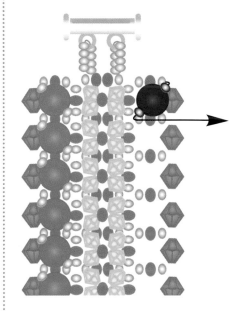

27 Pass through one C.

28 String one B. Pass through the next C. Repeat this all the way down your bracelet.

29 Pass through a few beads and finish off the thread. Unwind the thread from the bobbin. Thread a needle onto the other end and recondition the thread if necessary.

30 Repeat steps 27 to 29 to finish the bracelet.

You can put away your tools and any extra beads—your bracelet is ready to wear!

center of attraction necklace

Create a bead-dazzling bouquet of crystals and pearls with this lovely piece. First you'll weave a base, then glam it up with little crystals and seed beads. The last step is to bead a simple self-twisting neck chain from which to hang this attention-getter.

YOU'LL NEED

12 white opal crystal bicones, 4 mm (A)

Size 15° gold Japanese seed beads, 2 g (B)

8 white glass pearls, 4 mm (C)

4 gold aurum 2X crystal bicones, 3 mm (D)

12 crystal AB2X crystal bicones, 3 mm (E)

8 light gray opal AB2X crystal bicones, 3 mm (F)

Size 11° silver-lined light peach Japanese seed beads, 8 g (G)

Size 11° matte cream Japanese seed beads, 2 g (H)

FireLine, 6-pound test

Scissors

Thread conditioner (optional)

Size 12 or 13 beading needles

Plastic thread bobbin

Thread burner (optional)

Beading mat

Measuring tape

DIMENSIONS

28 inches (71.1 cm) long

DIFFICULTY LEVEL

Advanced

1 Cut and condition 2 yards (1.8 m) of thread. Wrap 22 inches (55.9 cm) of it onto a plastic thread bobbin. Thread a needle onto the other end. This tail thread will be used later to create the bail of your pendant. String one A and slide it down to the bobbin.

2 String one B, one A, one B, one C, one B, one A, and one B. Pass through the first A to form a square. Pass through one B, one A, one B, and one C.

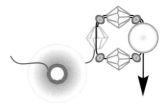

3 String one B, one C, one B, one C, one B, one C, and one B. Pass through one C to form a new square. In the new square, pass through one B and one C.

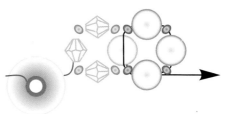

4 String one B, one A, one B, one A, one B, one A, and one B. Pass through one C to form a new square. In the pearl square, pass through one B and one C.

5 Repeat step 4 twice more. This completes the base of your pendant.

6 String one B, one D, one B, one D, and one B. Pass through the C you were coming out of to form a triangle. In the new triangle, pass through one B, one D, and one B.

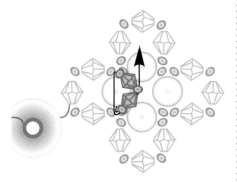

7 String three Bs. Pass through the B you were coming out of to form a small square. Continue to pass through the next B in the square.

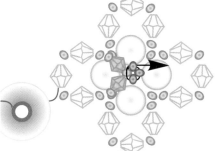

8 String one D and one B. Pass through one C. String one B.

Pass through one D from the last triangle and two Bs in the small square to build a second triangle.

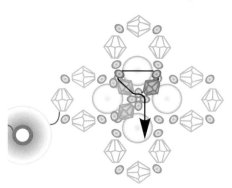

9 Repeat step 8 once more to create a third triangle.

10 Pass through one D from the first triangle. String one B. Pass through one C. String one B. Pass through one D from the third triangle to complete the fourth triangle. Pass through one B.

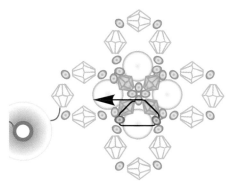

11 In the new triangle, continue to pass through one D, one B, and one C.

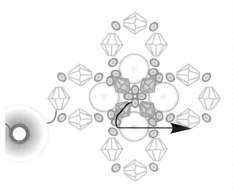

12 String one B, one E, one B, one E, and one B. Pass through the C

you were coming out of to form a new triangle.

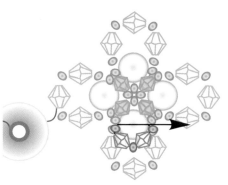

13 In the new triangle, pass through one B, one E, and one B.

14 String three Bs. Pass through the B you were coming out of to form a small square. Pass through the next B in the square.

15 String one F and one B. Pass through one A. String one B. Pass through one E from the last triangle. Continue to pass through two Bs in the small square.

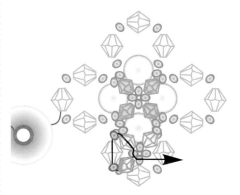

16 String one F and one B. Pass through one A. String one B. Pass through one F from the last triangle. Continue to pass through two Bs in the small square.

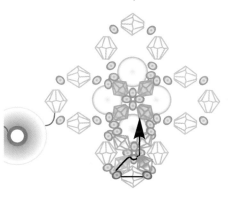

17 Pass through one E from the first triangle. String one B. Pass through one A. String one B. Pass through one F. This completes the fourth triangle.

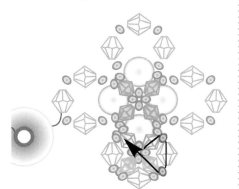

18 In the new triangle, pass through one B and one E. Continue to pass through one B, one C, one B, and one C. You should be directly across from your bobbin.

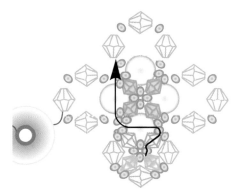

19 String one B, one E, one B, one E, and one B. Pass through the C you were coming out of to form a new triangle.

> **NOTE:** Step 19 is almost the same as step 12, except the thread path is in the opposite direction.

In the new triangle, pass through one B, one E, and one B.

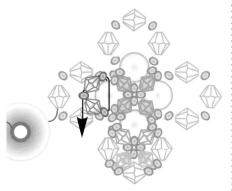

20 String three Bs. Pass through the B you were coming out of to form a small square. Pass through the next B in the square.

21 String one F and one B. Pass through one A. String one B. Pass through one E from the last triangle. Continue to pass through two Bs in the small square.

22 String one F and one B. Pass through one A. String one B. Pass through one F from the last triangle. Continue to pass through two Bs in the small square.

23 Pass through one E from the first triangle. String one B. Pass through one A. String one B. Pass through one F. This completes the fourth triangle.

24 Pass through two Bs in the small square. Continue to pass through one E, one B, one C, one B, and one C.

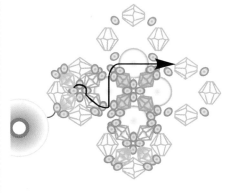

25 Repeat steps 19 to 24 to embellish a new square section of the base.

26 Repeat steps 19 to 23 to embellish the last section of the base.

27 Pass through three Bs in the small square. Continue to pass through one F, one B, one A, and one B.

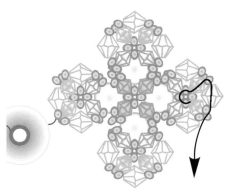

28 String one B, one C, and one B. Pass through one B, one A, and one B. Repeat this three more times, moving all the way around your pendant and keeping the tension tight.

Your pendant should be very three-dimensional now, almost like a dome. Pass through a few beads to tighten up any loose areas. Finish off the thread. Unwind the thread from the bobbin. Thread a needle onto the other end. Recondition thread if necessary.

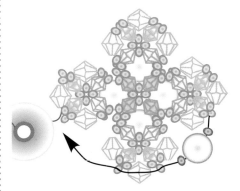

29 Pass through two Bs and one C.

30 String nine Gs. Pass through the C you were coming out of. Continue to pass through six Gs.

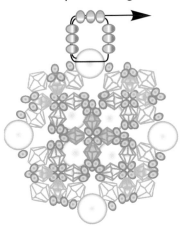

31 String seven Gs. Pass through the top three Gs from the last loop to create a rectangle.

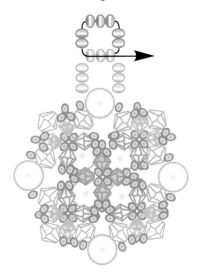

32 String one B, one E, and one B. Lay these strung beads diagonally over the rectangle. Pass through the top three Gs.

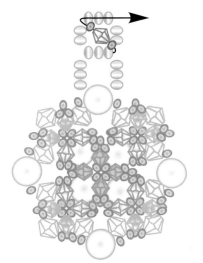

33 Repeat steps 31 and 32 three times.

34 String three Gs. Pass through one C. String three Gs. Pass through the three Gs from the last rectangle to complete the bail.

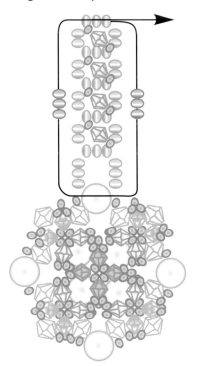

Use the remaining thread to pass through the beads and tighten up any loose areas. Finish off the thread.

35 Now you'll start making the beaded chain. Cut and condition whatever length of thread you feel comfortable with. (It's better to work with a comfortable length rather than get tangled up in a really long piece of thread.) Thread a needle onto one end.

36 String six Gs. Pass through the first G to form a circle. Position your circle approximately 6 inches (15.2 cm) from the far end. Pass through all six Gs again to secure its position on the thread. You should be exiting out of the G with the tail thread coming out of it.

37 String one B, one H, and one B. Lay these strung diagonally over your circle. Pass through the third G to get to the other side of the circle.

38 String five Gs. Pass through the G you were coming out of to form another circle.

39 Repeat steps 37 and 38 until the chain is long enough to pass over your head. Add new thread when necessary. Your beaded chain is supposed to twist, so don't try to correct it.

40 Repeat step 37 to embellish the last circle.

41 String on your pendant. String two Gs. Pass through the G that the tail thread is coming out of to start connecting the ends of your beaded chain together. String two Gs. Pass through the G from the last circle to complete the connection.

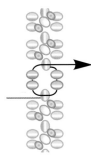

42 Repeat step 37 to embellish the last circle. Pass through a few beads. Finish off the thread. Thread a needle onto the tail thread and finish it off.

You're finished! Put on your necklace—it's time to go flaunt it!

curves

· · · · · · · · · · · · · · · ·

In this chapter, you'll learn two methods
of RAW to create curvature in beadwork.

FIGURE I

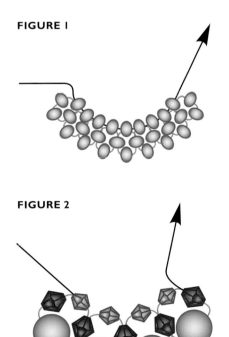

In the first, the curve is created simply by
passing through only the top edge of beads,
cinching up the gaps between them. This
creates the strip to bend (figure 1). This
method is used in the Poppy Ring (page 67).

FIGURE 2

In the other method, the beads on one
side of the row are much smaller than on
the opposite side. This causes the beaded
strip to flare out and curve (figure 2). This
technique is used in both the Egyptian
Queen Collar (page 70) and the Timeless
Drops Earrings (page 64) .

timeless drops earrings

Drops have always been a favorite shape in vintage jewelry. Using varied sizes of beads creates the curvature needed to form this timeless look. This design can also be adapted into a pendant for a necklace.

YOU'LL NEED

Size 11° seed bead

22 crystal golden shadow crystal bicones, 3 mm (A)

Size 15° gold Japanese seed beads, 1 g (B)

24 crystal bronze shade crystal bicones, 4 mm (C)

20 powder almond glass pearls, 3 mm (D)

2 crystal golden shadow crystal briolette top-drilled pendants, 11 x 5.5 mm (E)

2 wire guardians with 0.031-inch (0.8 mm) hole diameter

1 pair of French hook earring findings

FireLine, 6-pound test

Scissors

Thread conditioner (optional)

2 size 12 or 13 beading needles

Thread burner (optional)

Beading mat

Measuring tape

Chain-nose jewelry pliers

DIMENSIONS

1½ inches (3.8 cm)

DIFFICULTY LEVEL

Intermediate

1 Cut and condition 1 yard (91.4 cm) of thread. Thread a needle onto one end. String the size 11° seed bead and pass through it again to temporarily secure it so it serves as a stop bead. Slide it along the thread so it's 11 inches (27.9 cm) from the far end. String one A and slide it up against the stop bead.

2 String one B, one C, one B, one A, and one D. Pass through the A from the previous step to form a funny-shaped square, which will be referred to as a unit. Continue to pass through one B, one C, one B, and one A.

3 String one D, one A, one B, one C, and one B. Pass through one A from the last unit to create a new unit. In the new unit, pass through one D and one A.

4 Repeat steps 2 to 3 to make the third and fourth unit. Repeat step 2 to make the fifth unit.

5 String one B, one A, one B, one C, two Bs, one C, and one B. Pass through one A from the last unit to create the point of your teardrop. Continue to pass through one B and one A.

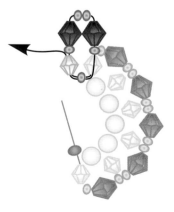

6 Repeat steps 2 to 3 two times.

7 String one B, one C, and one B. Pass through one A from the first unit (this is the A next to the stop bead). String one D. Pass through one A from the last unit to connect both ends. Leave this thread alone for now. It will be used later.

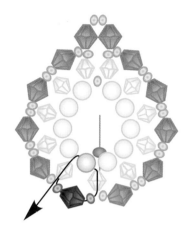

8 Remove the stop bead. Thread a needle onto the tail end. Pass through one D in the direction toward the point of the teardrop.

9 String one B. Pass through the next D. Repeat this three more times.

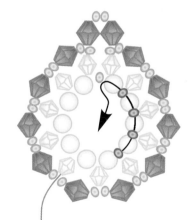

10 String one B. Pass through the next B at the bottom of the teardrop point. String one B and pass through the next D.

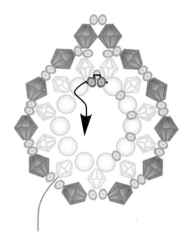

11 String one B. Pass through the next D. Repeat this four more times.

12 String one B. Skip over one B and pass through the next D. This new B should lie directly on top of the B already there. Repeat this three times.

13 Pass through three Bs. String one B, one E, and one B. Circle back and pass through the three Bs. Pass through the next D.

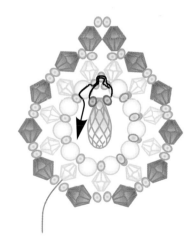

14 String one B. Skip over one B and pass through the next D. This new B should lie directly on top of the B already there. Repeat this four more times.

15 Pass through a few beads. Finish off the thread, and then go back to working with the main thread.

16 Pass through one B and one C in the direction toward the teardrop point.

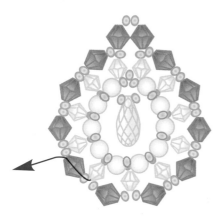

17 Pass through two Bs and one C. Repeat this two more times.

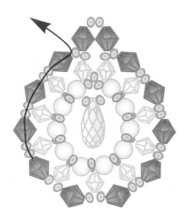

18 Pass through one B, one C, and two Bs at the top of the point. String one wire guard and pass through the two Bs again. Pass through the wire guard and the two Bs again to secure the guard's attachment. Continue to pass down the point through one C, one B, and one C.

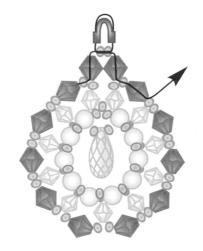

19 Pass through two Bs and one C. Repeat this five more times.

20 Use the remaining thread to pass through a few more outer beads to make the teardrop a little more rigid. Finish off the thread. Link an earring finding to the wire guard by opening and closing the earring's link with a pair of chain-nose pliers. One earring is done!

21 Repeat steps 1 through 20 to make the other earring.

You'll turn any outing into a red-carpet event when you wear these elegant earrings!

variation

With a few modifications to these instructions, I made a pendant to dangle from a pretty chain.

poppy ring

The poppy possesses a beautiful golden hue and, when it's in season, it blankets California's hillsides. This California state flower is quite resilient, surviving in dry climates and under a pounding sun. This design is my beaded interpretation of what the blossom means to me: beauty and strength.

YOU'LL NEED

Fire opal round crystal, 6 mm (A)

Size 11° peach Japanese seed beads, 1 g (B)

Size 11° raspberry AB Japanese seed beads, 1 g (C)

Size 8° light peach-lined clear seed beads, 2 g (D)

Size 15° orange silver-lined Japanese seed beads, 1 g (E)

14 crystal padparadscha AB2X bicones, 3 mm (F)

FireLine, 6-pound test

Scissors

Thread conditioner (optional)

Size 11 beading needles

Thread burner (optional)

Beading mat

Measuring tape

DIMENSIONS

Focal element, ¾ inch (7.6 cm) in diameter

DIFFICULTY LEVEL

Intermediate

1 You'll begin by making the poppy flower. Cut and condition 44 inches (1.1 m) of thread. Thread a needle onto one end. String one size 11° seed bead and pass through it again to temporarily secure it. Slide this stop bead down so it's 6 inches (15.2 cm) from the far end of the thread. String the A and position it next to the stop bead.

2 String six Bs. Pass through the A to outline one side of the crystal. String six Bs. Pass through the A again to outline the other side of the crystal.

3 Pass through six Bs. String one B. Pass through six Bs. String one B. Pass through one B. This eliminates the gaps in the outline above and below the bead hole of the crystal.

4 String three Bs. Pass through the B you were coming out of to form a square. Pass through the next B in the outline.

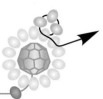

5 String two Bs. Pass through the B from the last square and two Bs in the outline. This creates a new square.

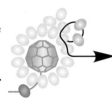

6 Repeat step 5 eleven times, making your way around the outline of B beads.

7 Pass through one B from the first square. String one B. Pass through one B from the last square made. This creates the 14th and final square. Pass through the B from the outline that you were coming out of and through two Bs in the new square.

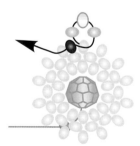

8 String one B, one D, and one B. Pass through the B you were coming out of to form a new square. String one C. Pass through the next B.

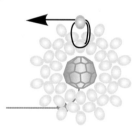

9 String one B and one D. Pass through the B from the last square and the B you were coming out of

to form a new square. String one C. Pass through the next B. The C beads should be poking upward toward what will be the front of your poppy, and the D beads should be lying toward the back.

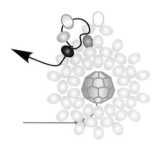

10 Repeat step 9 eleven times.

11 Pass through one B from the first square. String one D. Pass through one B from the last square. Pass through the B you were coming out of to complete the final square. String one C and pass through the next B.

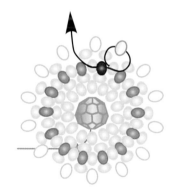

12 String three Es. Skip one C and pass through the next B. These new beads should sit beneath the C.

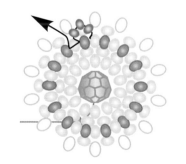

Repeat this step until you've added new beads under every C.

13 In the current square, pass through one B and one D.

14 String three Ds. Pass through the D you were coming out of to form a new square. String one C. Pass through the next D.

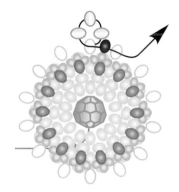

15 String two Ds. Pass through the D from the last square and the D you were coming out of to create a new square. String one C. Pass through the next D.

16 Repeat step 15 eleven times.

17 Pass through one D from the first square. String one D. Pass through one D from the last square and the D you were coming out of to complete the final square. String one C. Pass through one D. In that same square, continue to pass through two Ds to come out of the outer D.

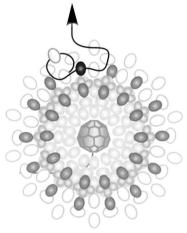

18 String one F. Pass through the next outer D. Repeat this all the way around your flower. Make sure the outer part of your flower cups upward.

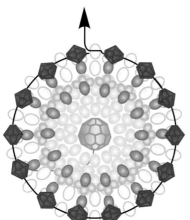

19 Pass through all the outer Ds and Fs with your remaining thread. (This will strengthen your beadwork and make it a little more rigid.) Tie several half-hitch knots along the way to maintain the bead tension you've created. After your last knot, finish off the thread.

20 Slide off the stop bead. Thread a needle onto the tail end. Flip your poppy over so you can work on the back. Pass through the Bs that outline the crystal to tighten up any loose areas, then finish off the thread. The poppy flower is complete.

21 Now you'll make the ring band. Cut and condition 44 inches (1.1 m) of thread, and thread it onto a needle. Add a stop bead and position it 6 inches (15.2 cm) from the tail end as you did before. Flip the poppy flower over to work on the back, and pass your needle through one C and one D.

22 String one C, three Bs, and one C. Pass through the D you were coming out of to form a circle. In that circle, pass through one C and three Bs.

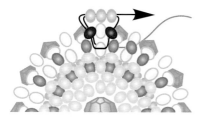

23 String one C, three Bs, and one C. Pass through the three Bs you were coming out of to form one unit. In that new unit, continue to pass through one C and three Bs.

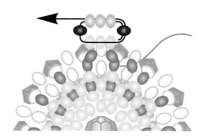

24 String one C, three Bs, and one C. Pass through the three Bs you were coming out of to form one unit. In that new unit, continue to pass through one C and three Bs.

25 Repeat steps 23 and 24 until the band is long enough to wrap around your finger.

26 To connect the band to the other side of the poppy, string one C. Pass through the D that's directly across from the D next to your stop bead. String one C. Pass through the three Bs you were coming out of from the last unit. This completes the joining unit.

27 In the joining unit, pass through one C, one D, and one C.

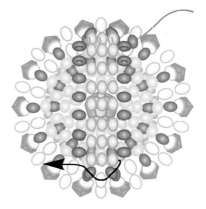

28 String one C. Pass through the next C. Repeat this all the way to the other end of the band.

29 Pass through one D and one C. Repeat step 28 to complete the other side of the band.

30 Pass through a few beads. Finish off the thread. Remove your stop bead. Thread a needle onto the tail end, and finish off the thread.

Time to enjoy the fruits of your labor—your poppy ring is ready to wear!

Back

egyptian queen collar

In designing this necklace, I was inspired by the beauty and allure of Egyptian queens such as Cleopatra and Nefertiti. Much ancient Egyptian artwork contains some aspect of the god Horus, who was often depicted as a hawk and shown either in full view or condensed down to just his wings. The scallops in this necklace fan out like wings and make anyone who wears it feel like a queen.

YOU'LL NEED

Size 15° silver-lined light blue Japanese seed beads, 5 g (A)

Size 15° nickel Japanese seed beads, 2 g (B)

Size 11° matte purple-gray Japanese seed beads, 7.5 g (C)

Size 8° light blue-gray seed beads, 8.5 g (D)

116 metallic blue 2X crystal bicones, 4 mm (E)

24 light gray glass pearls, 4 mm (F)

Montana AB round, 8 mm (G)

FireLine, 6-pound test

Scissors

Thread conditioner (optional)

Size 12 or 13 beading needles

Thread burner (optional)

Beading mat

Measuring tape

DIMENSIONS

17 inches (43.2 cm) long

DIFFICULTY LEVEL

Advanced

1 Cut and condition 2 yards (1.8 m) of thread. Thread a needle onto one end. String one size 11° seed bead to serve as a stop bead, and pass through it again to temporarily secure it. Slide it down until it's 6 inches (15.2 cm) from the far end. String one A and slide it down to your stop bead.

2 String three As. Pass through one A to form a square or unit.

3 String one B and three As. Pass through one A from the last unit to create one new unit. Skip one B and pass through one A in the new unit.

4 Repeat step 3 nine times to make a total of 11 units. This completes the first row. Pass through two As. String three Cs. Pass through one A to form a new unit. Continue to pass through one C.

5 String two Cs. Pass through one A from the previous row and one C from the last unit to form a new unit. In the new unit, pass through two Cs. Pass through the next A from the previous row.

6 String two Cs. Pass through one C from the last unit to form a new unit. Pass through one A and one C in the new unit.

7 Repeat steps 5 and 6 four times. You should have a total of 11 units. This completes the second row. Pass through one C.

8 String two Cs, one D, and two Cs. Pass through one C to form a new unit. In the new unit, continue to pass through two Cs.

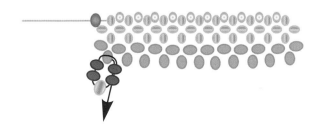

9 String one D and two Cs. Pass through one C from the previous row and two Cs from the last unit to form a new unit. In the new unit, pass through one D and two Cs. Continue to pass through the next C from the last row to prepare for the next new unit.

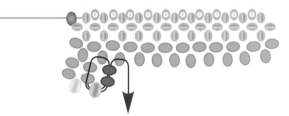

10 String two Cs and one D. Pass through two Cs from the last unit to form a new unit. In the new unit, continue to pass through three Cs.

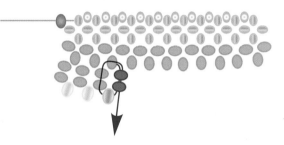

11 Repeat steps 9 and 10 four times. You should have a total of 11 units. This completes the third row.

12 String one B, one D, and one B. Lay the strung beads diagonally over the unit. Pass through two Cs of the next unit. Repeat this step for all remaining 10 units of this row.

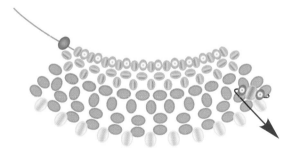

13 Pass through one D so that you are exiting out of the bottom of the third row.

14 String one A, one E, one A, one D, one A, one E, and one A. Pass through one D to form a new unit. Pass through one A, one E, and one A. String five As. Skip over one D. Pass through one A, one E, one A, one D, one A, and one E.

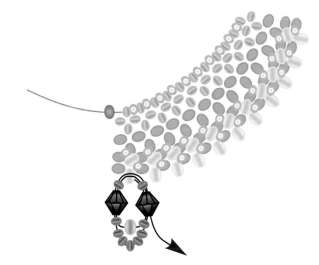

15 String one A, one D, one A, one E, and one A. Pass through the next D from the last row. String one A. Pass through one E from the last unit to form a new unit. Pass through one A. String five As. Skip over one D. Pass through one A and one E.

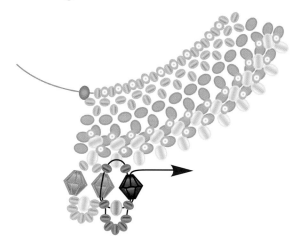

16 String one A. Pass through the next D from the last row. String one A, one E, one A, one D, and one A. Pass through one E from the last unit to form a new unit. In the new unit, continue to pass through one A, one D, one A, one E, and one A. String five As. Skip over one D and pass through one A, one E, one A, one D, one A, and one E.

17 Repeat steps 15 and 16 four times. You should have a total of 11 units with the bottom Ds outlined with As.

18 Continue to pass through four As. Leave this thread alone for now. Remove the stop bead. Thread a needle onto the tail end and finish it off. You've completed one fan shape.

19 Repeat steps 1 to 18 to make eight more fan shapes.

20 To begin connecting a pair of fan shapes, lay them on your work surface so that only one thread is between the two shapes. Thread a needle onto that thread. String one D. Pass through two As of the other fan shape. String one B. Pass through two As of the previous fan shape to make a triangle. In that triangle, continue to pass through one D, two As, and one B. Pass through two As and one E.

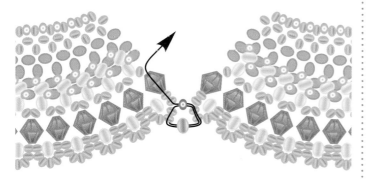

21 String one C, one E, and one C. Pass through one E and two As from the other fan shape. This creates a triangle. Continue to pass through one B, two As, one E, one C, and one E.

22 String one B, one C, one F, and one B. Pass through one B. String one B. Pass through one F. String one C and one B. Pass through one E to complete the embellishment over the triangle.

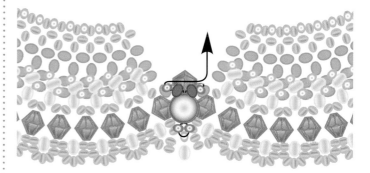

23 String one B, one F, and one B. Pass through one C at the edge of the second fan shape. String eight Bs. Pass through one B and one E. String one B, one F, and one B. Pass through one C at the edge of the second row of the other fan. String eight Bs. Pass through one B, one E, and two Bs.

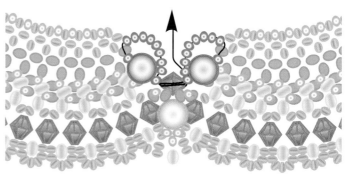

24 String four Bs. Skip over one E. Pass through two Bs, one E, and four Bs. String one B. Pass through four Bs to create a point at the top of the connection.

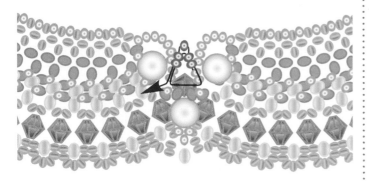

25 Pass through a few beads to tighten up any loose areas in the connection. Finish off the thread. Your connection is complete. You should have one thread remaining that is exiting out of the other fan shape.

26 Repeat steps 20 to 25 to attach all of the remaining fan shapes, making one long beaded strip. Be sure to finish off all remaining threads. You'll use new thread when attaching the beaded closure.

27 Cut and condition 16 inches (40.6 cm) of thread. Thread a needle onto one end. String one size 11° seed bead and pass through it again to temporarily secure it. This will be a stop bead. Position the stop bead approximately 6 inches (15.2 cm) from the far end. Pass through two Cs from the third row of the fan shape on either end.

28 String four Cs, one G, and three Bs. Pass back down through one G and one C. String three Cs. Pass through two Cs from the fan shape to create a triangle.

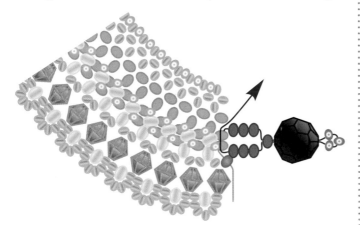

Pass through all the beads in the triangle to reinforce this attachment. Finish off the thread. Remove the stop bead and thread a needle onto the tail end. Finish off the thread.

29 Cut and condition 22 inches (55.9) of thread. Thread a needle onto one end. String one size 11° seed bead and pass through it again to temporarily secure it. (This will be a stop bead.) Position the stop bead approximately 6 inches (15.2 cm) from the far end. Pass through two Cs from the third row of the fan shape on the other end.

30 String five Cs. Pass through the two Cs from the third row to create a circle. Continue to pass through three Cs so that you're exiting out of the "peak bead."

31 String 17 Cs. Pass through the peak bead to form a new circle. Pass through the next C in the new circle.

32 String two Cs. Pass through one C from the last circle and two Cs in the new circle to form a small circle or unit. Repeat this 15 times. You should be one C short of completely going around the large circle.

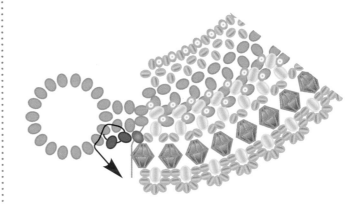

33 Pass through one C. String one C. Pass through one C from the last unit and the last C in the circle from which you were coming out initially. This completes the large circle.

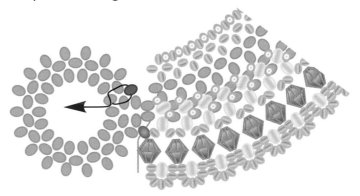

Pass through the inner 18 Cs that make up the large circle to tighten it. Finish off the thread.

Prepare to wow the masses because your necklace is ready to be shown off!

6

going tubular

There are two ways to form a tube with right angle weave.

Imagine being in a round building and circling the entire floor along the wall, only to find a staircase attached to the wall, which you then take to go to the next floor. Working in the round follows this approach, and figure 1 shows how. First, you make the first row and connect the first and last units to form a ring. Then you spiral upward, adding new rows. Bamboo Ring (page 76) is a perfect example of working in the round.

FIGURE I

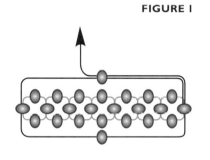

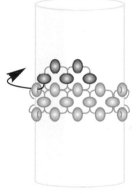

FIGURE 2

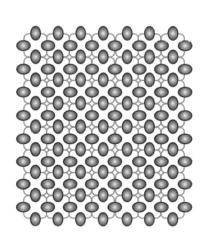

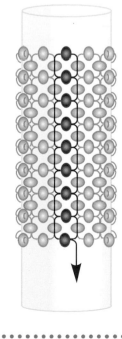

The simpler method is very much like rolling a sheet of paper into a tube. Make a flat beaded strip in the desired length, then join two parallel edges to form a cylinder. Figure 2 shows an example. Both the Bubble Pop Bracelet (page 79) and the Triple Elegance Lariat (page 84) use this method.

bamboo ring

Make something chic while learning tubular RAW. Part of bamboo's beauty lies in its structural simplicity and strength. This plant is the Chinese symbol of longevity. In India, it symbolizes friendship. May the wearer of this ring have long, beautiful friendships.

1 Cut and condition 2 yards (1.8 m) of thread. Thread a needle onto one end. String one size 11° bead and pass through it again to temporarily secure it. Slide this stop bead down to 6 inches (15.2 cm) from the far end. String two As.

2 String one B, two As, and one B. Pass through the first two As to form one unit. Make sure this first unit is positioned next to your stop bead. Continue to pass through one B and two As.

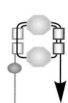

3 String one B, two As, and one B. Pass through the two As from the last unit to create a new unit. In the new unit, continue to pass through one B and two As.

4 Repeat steps 2 and 3 to add two more units. This is the front or focal point of the ring.

5 Now to start the band: string four As. Pass through the two As from the last unit to create a new unit. In the new unit, continue to pass through three As.

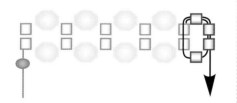

6 String four As. Pass through the two As from the last unit to create a new unit. In the new unit, pass through three As.

7 Continue to repeat steps 5 and 6 until your beaded strip is just one unit short of wrapping around the ring finger. Make sure you have an even number of units—this includes the units containing the glass beads (B).

8 String one A. Pass through the two As from the first unit. String one A. Pass through the two As from the last unit. This creates a new unit and completes the first row of your beaded tube. In the new unit, pass through one A.

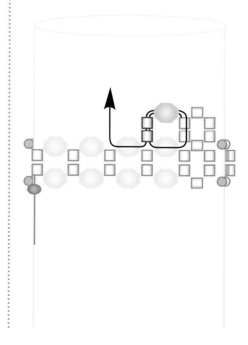

9 String five As. Pass through the one A you were coming out of to form the first unit of the new row. In the new unit, pass through two As.

10 String one B and two As. Pass through one B from the last row. Pass through two As from the last unit of the new row to create a new unit. In the new unit, pass through one B and two As. Pass through the next B of the last row.

11 String two As and one B. Pass through the two As from the last unit of the new row to create a new unit. Continue to pass through one B and two As of the new unit.

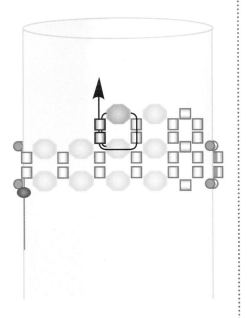

12 Repeat steps 10 and 11 to add two more units.

13 String three As. Pass through one A from the last row. Continue to pass through two As from the last unit of the new row. This creates a new unit. In the new unit, pass through three As. Continue to pass through the next A from the last row.

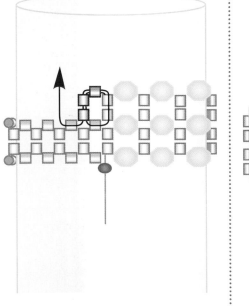

14 String three As. Pass through the two As from the last unit of the new row to create a new unit. In the new unit, pass through three As.

15 Continue to repeat steps 13 and 14 until you are one unit short of completing this new row.

16 Pass through one A from the last row and two As from the first unit of the new row. String one A. Pass through five As to create the last unit of the new row. This completes the new row. In the first unit of the newly completed row, pass through one A.

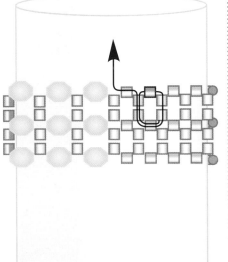

17 Repeat steps 9 to 16 two more times to add two more rows.

18 String one A. Pass through one B.

19 Repeat step 18 three times.

20 String one A. Pass through the top A of the next unit. Repeat this all the way around the rim of the beaded ring.

21 Pass through a few beads, then finish off the thread. Remove the stop bead. Thread a needle onto the tail end.

22 Pass through one B. Repeat step 18 three times.

23 Repeat steps 20 and 21 to complete the rim and finish off your thread.

Slip the ring on your finger, and make sure to use your hands a lot when you talk so people will notice your beautiful bauble.

bubble pop bracelet

When you weave a tube in RAW, the end result doesn't necessarily have to look like a tube. This beaded tube is actually a folded piece of RAW, which gives the piece more depth. The drop beads—glassy bubbles that add a pop of color—give even more dimension and texture to this fun bracelet.

YOU'LL NEED

Size 8° matte olive green Japanese seed beads, 18 g (A)

Size 15° bronze Japanese seed beads, 4 g (B)

3.4-mm raspberry gold luster drop beads, 9 g (C)

Two-strand slide clasp

FireLine, 6-pound test

Scissors

Thread conditioner (optional)

Size 11 beading needles

Thread burner (optional)

Beading mat

Measuring tape

DIMENSIONS

7¼ inches (18.4 cm) long

DIFFICULTY LEVEL

Intermediate

1 Cut and condition a length of thread you are comfortable working with. Thread a needle onto one end. String one size 11° seed bead and pass through it again to temporarily secure it. This is the stop bead. Slide it down so it's 6 inches (15.2 cm) from the far end. String one A and slide it next to the stop bead.

2 String one B, one A, one B, one A, one B, one A, and one B. Pass through the first A to form a circle. Continue to pass through one B, one A, and one B. One unit is made.

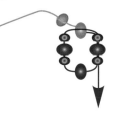

3 String one A, one B, one A, one B, and one A. Pass through one B, one A, and one B from the last unit to create a new unit. Continue to pass through one A, one B, one A, and one B in the new unit.

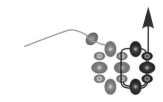

4 String one A, one B, one A, one B, and one A. Pass through one B, one A, and one B from the last unit to create a new unit. Continue to pass through one A, one B, one A, and one B in the new unit.

5 Repeat step 3 to create a fourth unit.

6 String one A, one B, one A, one B, and one C. Pass through one B, one A, and one B from the last unit to create a new unit. Continue to pass through one A, one B, one A, and one B in the new unit.

7 String one C, one B, one A, one B, and one A. Pass through one B, one A, and one B from the last unit to create a new unit. Continue to pass through one C, one B, one A, and one B in the new unit.

8 Repeat steps 6 and 7 to add two more units. Repeat step 4 to add an extra unit. In the new unit, continue to pass through the next A. This completes the first row.

9 String one B, one A, one B, one A, one B, one A, and one B. Pass through the A that you were originally coming out of to form the first unit of the new row. Continue to pass through one B, one A, and one B in the first unit.

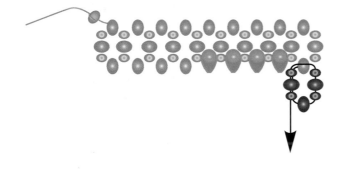

10 String one C, one B, one A, and one B. Pass through the next C from the previous row. Pass through one B, one A, and one B from the last unit to

create a new unit of the new row. Continue to pass through one C, one B, one A, and one B in the new unit. Pass through the next C from the previous row.

11 String one B, one A, one B, and one C. Pass through one B, one A, and one B from the last unit to create a new unit. Continue to pass through one C, one B, one A, and one B in the new unit.

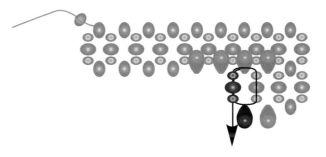

12 Repeat steps 10 and 11 to add two more units. Make sure your drop beads are pointing out on the same side of your bracelet. This will be the front of your bracelet.

13 String one A, one B, one A, and one B. Pass through the next A from the previous row. Pass through one B, one A, and one B from the last unit to create a new unit. Continue to pass through one A, one B, one A, and one B in the new unit. Pass through the next A from the previous row.

14 String one B, one A, one B, and one A. Pass through one B, one A, and one B from the last unit to create a new unit. Continue to pass through one A, one B, one A, and one B in the new unit.

15 Repeat steps 13 and 14 to add two more units. Continue to pass through one A in the new unit. This completes row 2.

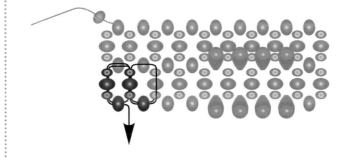

16 String one B, one A, one B, one A, one B, one A, and one B. Pass through the A that you were originally coming out of to form the first unit of the new row. Continue to pass through one B, one A, and one B in the first unit.

17 String one A, one B, one A, and one B. Pass through the next A from the previous row. Pass through one B, one A, and one B from the last unit to create a new unit. Continue to pass through one A, one B, one A, and one B in the new unit.

18 Pass through the next A from the previous row. String one B, one A, one B, and one A. Pass through one B, one A, and one B from the last unit to create a new unit. Continue to pass through one A, one B, one A, and one B in the new unit.

19 Repeat step 17 to add a new unit.

20 Pass through the next C from the previous row. String one B, one A, one B, and one C. Pass through one B, one A, and one B from the last unit to create a new unit. Continue to pass through one C, one B, one A, and one B in the new unit.

21 String one C, one B, one A, and one B. Pass through the next C from the previous row. Pass through one B, one A, and one B from the last unit to create a new unit. Continue to pass through one C, one B, one A, and one B in the new unit.

22 Repeat steps 20 and 21 to add two new units. Repeat step 18 to add an extra unit. Continue to pass through one A in the new unit. This completes row 3.

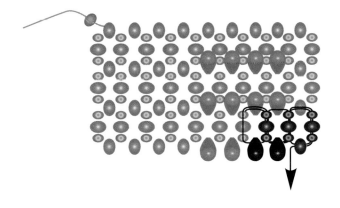

23 Repeat steps 9 to 22 to add more rows. Leave approximately a ¼-inch (6 mm) gap for the clasp. Make sure you finish with an odd number of rows.

24 Repeat step 9 to create the first unit of a new row.

25 String one A, one B, one A, and one B. Pass through the next C from the last row. Pass through one B, one A, and one B from the last unit to create a new unit. Continue to pass through one A, one B, one A, and one B in the new unit. Pass through the next C from the last row.

26 String one B, one A, one B, and one A. Pass through one B, one A, and one B from the last unit to create a new unit. Continue to pass through one C, one B, one A, and one B in the new unit.

27 Repeat steps 25 and 26 to add two more units.

28 String one A, one B, one A, and one B. Pass through the next A from the last row. Pass through one B, one A, and one B from the last unit to create a new unit. Continue to pass through one A, one B, one A, and one B in the new unit. Pass through the next A from the last row.

29 String one B, one A, one B, and one A. Pass through one B, one A, and one B from the last unit to create a new unit. Continue to pass through one A, one B, one A, and one B in the new unit.

30 Repeat steps 28 and 29 to complete the new row.

31 Now, you will begin to join the sides together to form a tube. Flip your beaded strip to the back. String one A. Pass through one B, one A, and one B on the other side of the row. String one A. Pass through one B, one A, and one B from where you came out of to create a new unit. In the new unit, continue to pass through one A, one B, one A, one B, and one A.

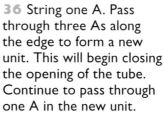

32 Pass through one B, one A, and one B in the next row. String one A. Pass through one B, one A, and one B from the other side of the row. Continue to pass through one A from the last unit to create a new unit. In the new unit, continue to pass through one B, one A, one B, and one A.

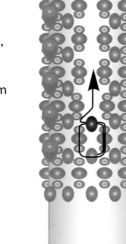

33 Pass through one B, one A, and one B in the next row. String one A. Pass through one B, one A, and one B from the other side of the row. Continue to pass through one A from the last unit to create a new unit. In the new unit, continue to pass through one B, one A, one B, and one A.

34 Continue to repeat steps 32 and 33 all the way down your bracelet.

35 Pass through the next two As along the edge.

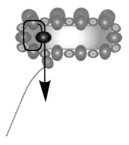

36 String one A. Pass through three As along the edge to form a new unit. This will begin closing the opening of the tube. Continue to pass through one A in the new unit.

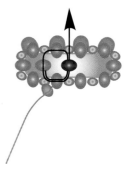

37 Pass through one A. String one A. Pass through two As to form a new unit. Continue to pass through two As in the new unit.

38 Pass through one A. String one A. Pass through two As to form a new unit. Continue to pass through two As in the new unit.

39 Pass through the three As on the edge. Pass through four As to complete the closing of the tube at this end.

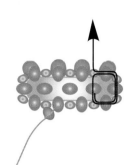

40 String one A, five Bs, one side of a clasp end, and one A. Pass through three As along the edge. Pass through one A, five Bs, the clasp end, and four As to reinforce the attachment to the clasp.

41 Pass through eight As so that you are coming out of the opposite side of the beaded tube.

42 Repeat step 40 to attach the other side of the clasp end.

43 Pass through a few beads. Finish off the thread. If you have any tail threads left over, remove their stop beads. Thread a needle onto one and finish off the tail threads one at a time until there are no more threads left.

44 Cut and condition 22 inches (55.9 cm) of thread. Thread a needle onto one end. Add one stop bead and position it 6 inches (15.2 cm) from the far end. Pass through three As along the edge at the other end of the tube.

45 Repeat steps 36 to 43 to close the tube and attach the other clasp end.

Needles down—your bracelet is complete!

Back

triple elegance lariat

Elegant and full of sparkle, this beaded lariat dresses up any outfit. Make a three-sided rope and embellish it with a variety of beads. Then, weave a very lush fringe of glass daggers to complete the look.

YOU'LL NEED

Size 11° matte amethyst AB Japanese seed beads, 14 g (A)

Size 10° topaz AB Japanese triangle beads, 15 g (B)

Size 15° grape Japanese seed beads, 6 g (C)

210 purple luster fire-polished glass beads, 3 mm (D)

216 amethyst AB2X crystal bicones, 3 mm (E)

6 cyclamen opal round beads, 4 mm (F)

6 pale lilac and silver dotted glass top-drilled daggers, 5 x 16 mm (G)

38 transparent lilac glass top-drilled daggers, 3 x 10 mm (H)

FireLine, 6-pound test

Scissors

Thread conditioner (optional)

Size 12 beading needles

Plastic thread bobbin

Thread burner (optional)

Beading mat

Measuring tape

DIMENSIONS

1 yard (91.4 cm) long

DIFFICULTY LEVEL

Advanced

1 Cut and condition a length of thread you are comfortable working with, plus an additional 1½ yards (1.4 m). Wrap 1½ (1.4 m) yards onto your bobbin. This thread will be used later to attach the fringe at the end. Thread a needle onto one end. String two As and slide them down to your bobbin.

2 String one B, two As, and one B. Pass through the first two As to form a square.

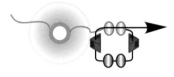

3 String one C, one B, and one C. Lay diagonally over the square and pass through the next two As. One new unit is complete.

4 Repeat step 2. String one C, one D, and one C. Lay diagonally over the square and pass through the next two As. One new unit is complete.

5 Repeat steps 2 and 3.

6 Repeat step 2. String one C, one E, and one C. Lay diagonally over the square and pass through the next two As. One new unit is complete.

7 Continue to repeat steps 2 through 6 until you've reached your desired length.

TIP: If you want a spiral look to your lariat, then make sure your second to last unit is embellished with C + E + C and the last unit is embellished with C + B + C.

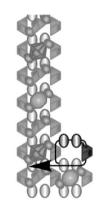

8 Pass through one B. This completes the first row.

9 String two As, one B, and two As. Pass through the B you were coming out of to form a new unit of the new row. In the new unit, continue to pass through two As, one B, and two As.

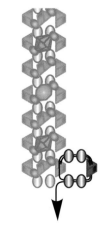

10 String one C, one D, and one C. Lay diagonally over the unit and pass through the next two As. One unit is complete.

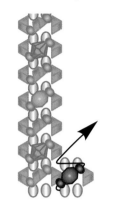

11 Pass through the next B from the last row. String two As and one B. Pass through the two As from the last unit to create a new unit.

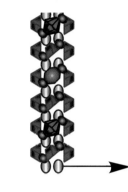

12 String one C, one B, and one C. Lay diagonally over the unit and pass through the next two As. One unit is complete.

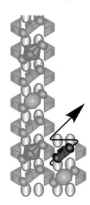

13 Repeat step 11. String one C, one E, and one C. Lay diagonally over the unit and pass through the next two As. One unit is complete.

14 Repeat steps 11 and 12.

15 Repeat step 11. Repeat step 10 to add a new unit.

16 Continue to repeat steps 11 to 15 to build new units onto the last row. This will complete the second row. Pass through one B, two As, and one B in that last unit.

17 Hold your strip, folded. You will now zip the sides closed to form a three-sided tube. String two As. Pass through one B opposite from where you are coming out of. String two As. Pass through the B you were originally coming out of to form a new unit. Continue to pass through two As in the new unit.

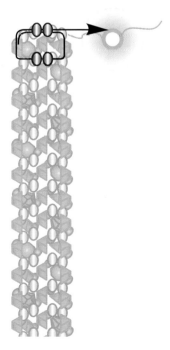

18 String one C, one B, and one C. Lay diagonally over the unit and pass through the next two As. One unit is complete.

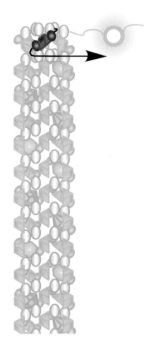

19 Pass through one B. String two As. Pass through one B on the opposite side. Pass through the two As from the last unit to create a new unit.

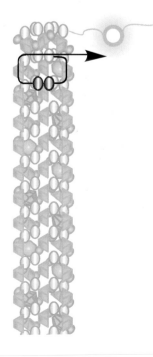

20 String one C, one E, and one C. Lay diagonally over the unit and pass through the next two As. One unit is complete.

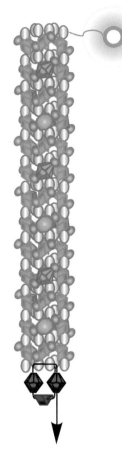

21 Repeat step 19. Repeat step 18. One new unit is complete.

22 Repeat step 19. String one C, one D, and one C. Lay diagonally over the unit and pass through the next two As. One unit is complete.

23 Repeat step 21.

24 Continue to repeat steps 19 to 23 until you've connected all of the Bs on the edges to form a tube.

25 String one E, one B, and one E. Pass through the two As you were coming out of to form a square. Pass through one E.

26 String one B and one E. Pass through the next two As and the E from the last square to create a new square. In the new square, continue to pass through one B and one E.

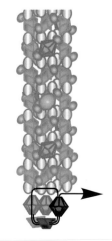

27 Pass through the next two As and one E from the first square. String one B. Pass through the E from the last square and the two As you were coming out of to complete the third square. Continue to pass through one E and one B in that new square.

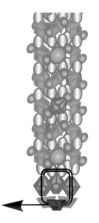

28 String one A. Pass through the next B. Repeat this two more times.

29 String one F, one B, and one F. Pass through the B you were coming out of to form a square. Pass through one A and one B.

30 String one F and one B. Pass through one F from the last square and the B you were originally coming out of to form a new square. Continue to pass through one A and one B.

31 Pass through one F. String one B. Pass through the previous F and the B you were originally coming out of to complete the third square. In the new square, continue to pass through one F and one B.

32 Repeat step 28.

33 String three As. Pass through the B you were coming out of to form a clover or unit. Continue to pass through two As.

34 String three As. Pass through the A from the last unit to create a new unit. Continue to pass through two As in the new unit. String three As. Pass through the A from the last unit to create a new unit. Continue to pass through two As in the new unit.

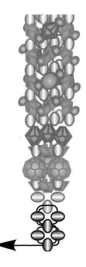

35 String one A, two Cs, one G, two Cs, and one A. Pass through the A from the last unit to create a new unit.

Continue to pass through two As in the same unit.

36 String one A, one C, one H, one C, and one A. Pass through the A you were originally coming out of to form a loop. Continue to pass through two As in the next unit, moving toward the beaded tube.

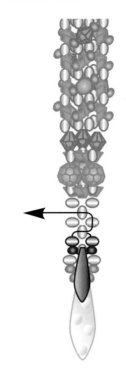

37 String one A, one C, one H, one C, and one A. Pass through the A you were originally coming out of to form a loop. Continue to pass through one A and one B in the next unit.

38 String two Cs, one H, and two Cs. Pass through the B you were originally coming out of to form a loop. Continue to pass across through one A.

39 String three As. Pass through the A you were originally coming out of to create a new unit.

Continue to pass through two As in the new unit.

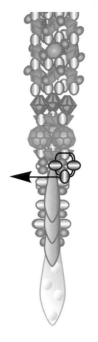

40 String three As. Pass through the A you were originally coming out of to create a new unit. Continue to pass through two As in the new unit.

41 String one A, one C, one H, one C, and one A. Pass through the A you were originally coming out of to form a loop. Continue to pass through two As from the last unit.

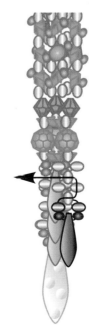

42 String one A, one C, one H, one C, and one A. Pass through the A you were originally coming out of to form a loop. Continue to pass through two As from the previous unit.

43 String two Cs, one H, and two Cs. Pass through the A you were coming out of to form a loop. Pass through the next B.

44 Repeat steps 33 through 43 to add two more branches of fringe.

45 Repeat steps 33 and 34. Repeat step 34 to make this branch longer than the others.

46 Repeat step 35.

47 Repeat step 36 three times.

48 Repeat steps 37 to 43 to finish the branch and add the final branch to complete the fringe.

49 Pass through a few beads, then finish off the thread.

50 Unwind the thread from the bobbin. Thread a needle onto this end and condition the thread if necessary. Finish the other end of the lariat with fringe by repeating steps 25 to 49.

Now for the fun part—wear your new necklace!

7

polygon stitch, a variation of RAW

. . . .

Hopefully at this point you've gotten the hang of RAW. You understand that each unit has the same number of sides and that the thread path goes either clockwise or counterclockwise. But what happens if the unit has only three sides, instead of four? You now have polygon stitch, which is sometimes referred to as triangle stitch.

FIGURE 1   **FIGURE 2**

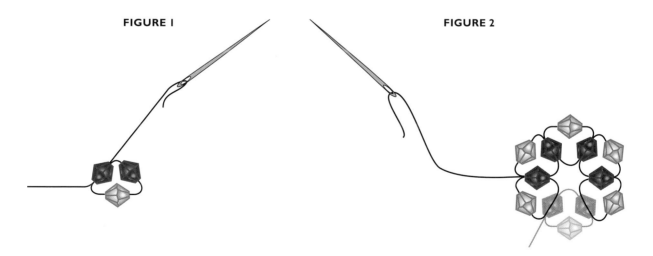

The same principles apply, where the thread path is either clockwise or counterclockwise (figure 1).

However, instead of a grid of squares, the units are triangles. Picture a round pie and each slice is a triangle (figure 2). In beadwork, these circles are transformed into flowers, as seen in Sparkling Blossoms Bracelet & Matching Ring (page 100) and Sunny Flowers Earrings (page 97).

marquis pendant

Using triangle weave stitch, you'll create an intricate pattern of triangles to form a marquis shape topped off with a pearl center. Complete the project by using traditional RAW to make a simple yet elegant beaded neck chain.

YOU'LL NEED

16 crystal silver shade crystal bicones, 3 mm (A)

Size 15° nickel Japanese seed beads, 2 g (B)

54 crystal silver night crystal bicones, 3 mm (C)

White glass pearl, 4 mm (D)

Size 11° silver-lined gray seed beads, 3 g (E)

Clasp

FireLine, 6-pound test

Scissors

Thread conditioner (optional)

Size 13 beading needles

Plastic thread bobbin

Thread burner (optional)

Beading mat

Measuring tape

DIMENSIONS

19 inches (48.3 cm) long

DIFFICULTY LEVEL

Intermediate

Pendant

1 Cut and condition 1½ yards (1.4 m) of thread. Thread a needle onto one end. String one size 11° seed bead. Pass through it again to temporarily secure it. This serves as a stop bead. Position it 6 inches (15.2 cm) from the far end. String one A and slide it next to the stop bead.

2 String one B, one C, one B, one C, and one B. Pass through one A to create a triangle. Continue to pass through one B, one C, and one B.

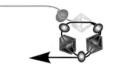

3 String five Bs. Pass through the B you were originally coming out of to form a circle. Pass through the next B in the circle.

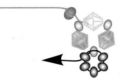

4 String one C, one B, one A, and one B. Pass through the C from the last triangle to create a new triangle. Pass through the B you were originally coming out of and the next B in the circle.

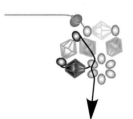

5 String one C, one B, one C, and one B. Pass through the C from the last triangle to create a new triangle. Pass through the B you were originally coming out of and the next B in the circle.

6 String one C, one B, one D, and one B. Pass through the C from the last triangle to create a new triangle. Pass through the B you were originally coming out of and the next B in the circle.

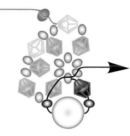

7 Repeat step 5 to add one new triangle.

8 Pass through one C from the first triangle. String one B, one A, and one B. Pass through the C from the last triangle to complete the new triangle. In the last triangle, pass through one B, one C, and one B.

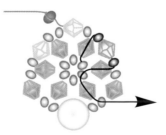

9 String four Bs. Pass through two Bs to form a circle. Pass through the next B in the circle.

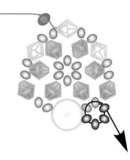

10 String one C, one B, one A, and one B. Pass through one C from the last triangle to create a new triangle. Pass through the B you were originally coming out of in the circle and the next B in the circle.

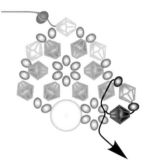

11 Repeat step 10 to add one new triangle.

12 String one C, one B, one C, and one B. Pass through one C from the last triangle to create a new triangle. Pass through the B you were originally coming out of in the circle and the next B in the circle.

13 Pass through one D. String one B, one C, and one B. Pass through the C from the last triangle to complete the new triangle. In the new triangle, pass through one B, one D, and one B.

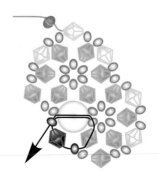

14 String three Bs. Pass through three Bs to form a circle. Pass through the next B in the circle.

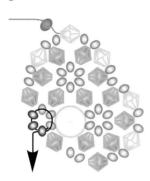

15 Repeat step 12 to add a new triangle.

16 Repeat step 10 to add a new triangle.

17 Pass through the next C. String one B, one A, and one B. Pass through the C from the last triangle to complete the new triangle. In the last triangle, pass through one B and one C. Continue to move down and pass through one B, one C, and the three Bs at the bottom.

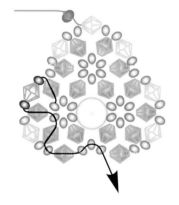

18 String three Bs. Pass through three Bs to form a circle. Pass through the next B in the circle.

19 Repeat step 10 two times to add two new triangles.

20 Pass through the next C. String one B, one A, and one B. Pass through the C from the last triangle to complete the new triangle. In the new triangle, pass through one

B. Continue to pass through one B, one C, and two Bs.

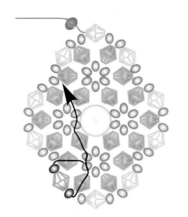

21 String five Bs. Skip over the D and pass through two Bs. Repeat to complete the outline around the D.

22 Pass through three Bs. String one B. Pass through one B. String one B. Pass through eight Bs. String one B. Pass through one B. String one B. Pass through four Bs, one C, one B, and one A.

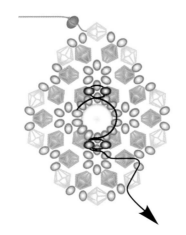

23 String two Bs. Pass through the next A. Repeat. These new beads should be underneath your beadwork.

24 String one B, one A, and one B. Pass through the next A. String two Bs. Pass through the next A. Repeat.

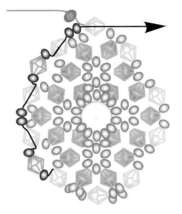

25 String one A, one E, and one A. Pass through the A you were originally coming out of to form a triangle.

26 String one B. Pass through one A. String five Bs. Skip over the E and pass through one A. String one B. Pass through one A.

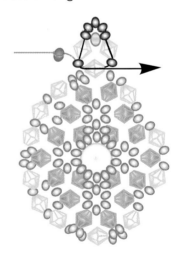

27 String two Bs. Pass through the next A. String one B, one A, and one B. Pass through the next A. Repeat.

28 Pass through a few beads, finish off the thread, and remove the stop bead. Thread a needle onto the tail end and finish off this thread. Your pendant is finished.

Neck Chain

1 Cut and condition 4 yards (3.7 m) of thread. Wrap half of the thread onto a bobbin. Thread a needle onto the other end. Pass through the five Bs at the point of the pendant.

2 String one E, two Bs, and one E. Pass through the two Bs you were coming out of from the pendant to create a circle or unit. Continue to pass through one E and two Bs.

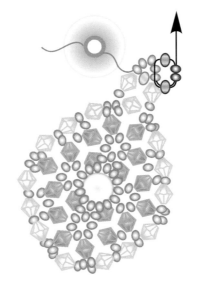

3 String one E, two Bs, and one E. Pass through two Bs from the last unit to create a new unit. Continue to pass through one E and two Bs.

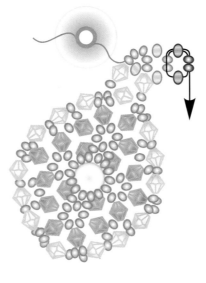

4 Repeat step 2 from the Neck Chain instructions to add a new unit.

5 String one C, two Bs, and one C. Pass through two Bs from the last unit to create a new unit. Continue to pass through one C and two Bs.

6 Repeat step 2 from the Neck Chain instructions three times.

7 Repeat steps 5 and 6 from the Neck Chain instructions eight times.

8 Repeat step 3 from the Neck Chain instructions until you've reached the desired length.

9 String two Bs, one E, and one clasp end. Pass back down through one E. String two Bs. Pass through the two Bs from the last unit to create a triangle. Pass through the beads and the clasp end in the triangle to reinforce the attachment of the clasp end.

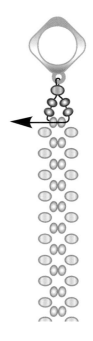

10 Pass through a few beads and finish off the thread.

11 Unwind thread from the bobbin. Thread a needle onto one end. Repeat steps 2 to 10 from the Neck Chain instructions to create the other half of the beaded neck chain.

spicy blossoms bracelet

Reminiscing about a visit to Sedona, Arizona, I couldn't help but dream up something in a desert palette. Blossoming desert plants add to the town's mystical charm. Considering Sedona's climate, it's no wonder those flowers come in hot and spicy shades! Weave this exotic floral bracelet with one needle and a variation of the RAW stitch.

YOU'LL NEED

44 copper round pearls, 4 mm (A)

Size 15° red seed beads, 2 g (B)

44 crystal copper crystal bicones, 4 mm (C)

Size 11° bright copper seed beads, 1 g (D)

40 turquoise AB crystal bicones, 3 mm (E)

20 crystal dorado crystal bicones, 4 mm (F)

Single-strand clasp

FireLine, 6 pound test

Scissors

Thread conditioner (optional)

Size 11 or 12 beading needles

Plastic thread bobbin

Thread burner (optional)

Beading mat

Measuring tape

DIMENSIONS

7¾ inches (19.7 cm) long

DIFFICULTY LEVEL

Intermediate

1 Cut and condition 5 yards (4.6 m) of thread. Wrap half of the thread onto your bobbin. Thread a needle onto the other end. String one A and slide it next to your bobbin.

2 String one B, one C, one D, one C, and one B. Pass through the A your thread is exiting out of to form the first triangle.

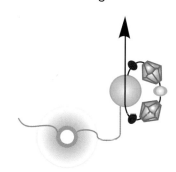

3 Pass through one B, one C, and one D.

4 String three Ds. Pass through the D your thread was exiting to form a clover.

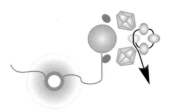

5 Pass through the next D in the clover.

6 String one C, one B, one A, and one B. Pass through the C from the last triangle and the D you started out from to form a second triangle. Pass through the next D in the clover.

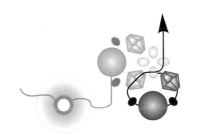

7 Repeat step 6 to form the third triangle.

8 Pass through the C from the first triangle.

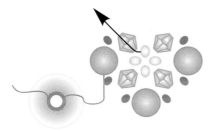

9 String one B, one A, and one B. Pass through the C from the third triangle to complete the fourth triangle. Continue to pass through

the D from your new triangle. At this point your beadwork should be a little mound. Do not pinch this flat between your fingers.

10 String one B and pass through the next D. Repeat this three more times.

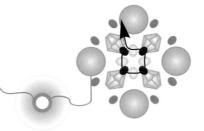

11 Pass down through one C, one B, and one A, working away from the bobbin.

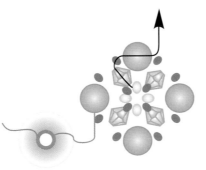

12 String three Bs, one E, and three Bs. Pass through the same A to outline it. Pass through two Bs and one A.

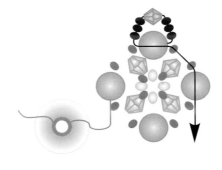

13 String three Bs, one E, and three Bs. Pass through the same A to outline it. Pass through two Bs, one A, two Bs, one A, two Bs, one A, three Bs, and one E. One blossom is made.

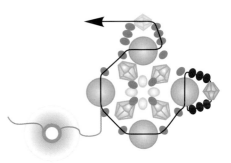

14 String one B, one F, one B, one E, and one D. Pass through the E you were exiting to form a triangle.

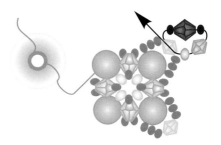

15 Pass through one B, one F, one B, and one E.

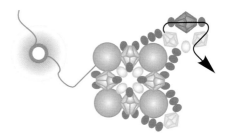

16 String three Bs, one A, and three Bs. Pass through the E you were exiting to form a new triangle.

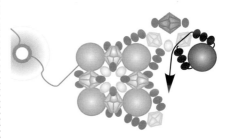

17 Pass through three Bs and one A.

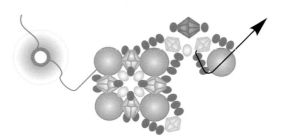

18 Repeat steps 2 to 11 to start the next blossom.

19 Repeat step 12 twice.

20 String three Bs, one E, and three Bs. Pass through the same A to outline it.

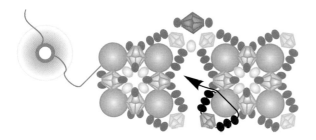

21 In the same outline, pass through three Bs and one E.

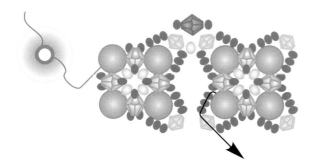

22 String one B, one F, and one B. Pass through the E from the last blossom. String one D. Pass through the E from the new blossom to create a new triangle.

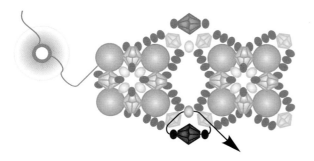

23 Pass through three Bs, one A, two Bs, one A, two Bs, one A, three Bs, and one E. You've completed a new blossom.

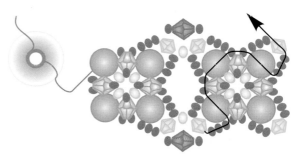

24 Repeat steps 14 to 23 three times. You should have a total of five blossoms.

25 Repeat steps 14 to 17.

26 Repeat steps 2 to 11 to start the next blossom.

27 Continue to pass through two Bs, one A, two Bs, and one A.

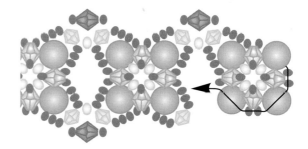

28 Repeat steps 20 to 22.

29 Pass through three Bs, one A, two Bs, one A, two Bs, one A, and two Bs.

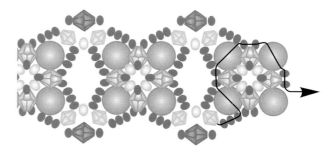

30 String two Bs, one D, and one clasp end. Pass back down through one D. String two Bs. Pass across through the two Bs you were exiting to create a triangle. Pass through all of the beads and clasp end in the triangle to reinforce the clasp attachment.

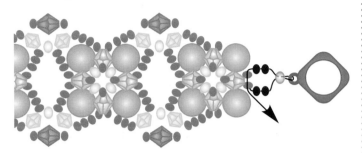

31 Pass through a few beads. Finish off the thread. Half of the bracelet is finished.

32 Unwind the thread from the bobbin. Thread a needle onto this end.

33 Flip your piece so that the thread exits the bottom of the blossom.

34 String three Bs, one E, and three Bs. Pass through the A you are exiting to outline the bead. Continue to pass through two Bs and one A.

35 String three Bs, one E, and three Bs. Pass through the A you are exiting to outline this bead.

36 Pass through one B, one C, one D, one C, one B, one A, two Bs, one A, three Bs, and one E.

37 Continue to repeat steps 14 to 23 until you're ¾ inch (1.9 cm) from the desired length.

38 Repeat steps 25 to 31 to finish your bracelet and add the other clasp end.

With the bracelet now completed, it's time to get spicy!

Back

sunny flowers earrings

YOU'LL NEED

32 padparadscha AB2X crystal
   bicones, 3 mm (A)

Size 15° metallic light peach Japanese
   seed beads, 1 g (B)

Size 11° matte transparent peach
   Japanese seed beads, 1 g (C)

2 powder almond glass pearls,
   4 mm (D)

2 wire guards

1 pair of French hook earring findings

FireLine, 6-pound test

Scissors

Thread conditioner (optional)

Size 11 beading needles

Plastic thread bobbin

Thread burner (optional)

Beading mat

Measuring tape

Chain-nose jewelry pliers

DIMENSIONS

1½ inches (3.8 cm)

DIFFICULTY LEVEL

Intermediate

There's nothing like beautiful flowers to brighten up your day. Using triangle stitch and some simple embellishing, you can transform crystals and beads into something truly exquisite!

1 Cut and condition 1 yard (91.4 cm) of thread. Wrap 22 inches (55.9 cm) of thread onto a bobbin. Thread a needle onto the other end. String one A and slide it down to the bobbin.

2 String one B, one A, one C, one A, and one B. Pass through the A you originally came out of to create a triangle.

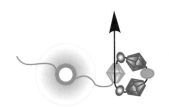

3 In the new triangle, pass through one B and one A.

4 String one C, one A, one B, one A, and one B. Pass through the A from the last triangle to create a new triangle.

5 In the new triangle, pass through one C and one A.

6 String one B, one A, one B, one A, and one C. Pass through the A from the last triangle to create a new triangle. In the new triangle, pass through one B, one A, one B, and one A.

7 Repeat steps 4 to 6 two times to add four new triangles.

8 String one C. Pass through one A from the first triangle. String one B, one A, and one B. Pass through the A you were originally coming out of to complete the eighth triangle.

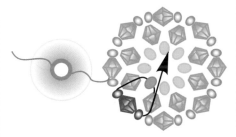

9 In the new triangle, pass through one C. String one D. Skip three Cs and pass through the fourth C. Pass through one D and the C you were originally coming out of to attach D to the center of the circle.

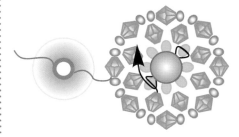

10 String one B. Pass through the next C. Repeat this seven times, inserting one B between all of the Cs.

11 Pass through one B.

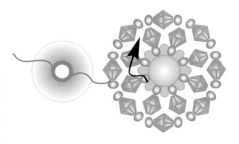

12 String three Bs. Skip over one C and pass through the next B.

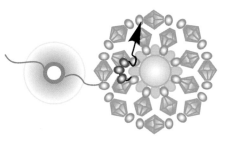

13 Repeat step 12 seven times to outline the rest of the Cs. Pass through a few beads. Finish off the thread. Unwind thread from the bobbin. Thread a needle onto this end. Pass through two Bs.

14 String five Bs. Skip over one A and pass through the next two Bs.

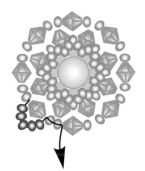

15 Repeat step 14 seven more times to outline the rest of the As.

16 Continue to pass through the next three As to exit out of the peak A.

17 String eight As. Pass through the peak A to form a circle. Continue to pass through five As. Now you are exiting out of the top two As in the circle.

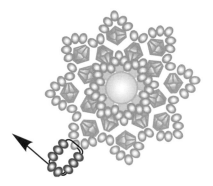

18 String one C, two As, and one C. Pass through the top two As from the last circle to create a small circle. Continue to pass through one C and two As.

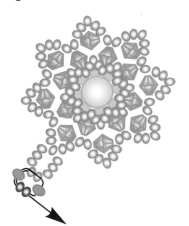

19 String one wire guard. Pass through the top two As. Reinforce this area by passing through the wire guard and the two As again.

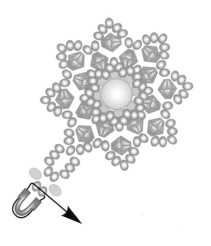

20 Pass through a few beads. Finish off the thread. With your chain-nose pliers, twist the link open on the earring finding to link it to the wire guard. Twist the link closed to secure the connection between the finding and the wire guard. One earring is done.

21 Repeat steps 1 to 20 to create another earring to complete the pair.

Don't these beaded bouquets look pretty on?

Back

sparkling blossoms bracelet & matching ring

YOU'LL NEED

30 aqua AB fire-polished beads, 4 mm (A)

24 light blue opal polished beads, 4 mm (B)

26 aqua gold-lined fire-polished beads, 4 mm (C)

30 deep blue-green fire-polished beads, 4 mm (D)

112 platinum gray glass pearls, 4 mm (E)

Size 11° metallic light peach Japanese seed beads, 3 g (F)

Single-strand clasp

Nylon beading thread

Scissors

Thread conditioner (optional)

Size 11 beading needles

Thread burner (optional)

Beading mat

Measuring tape

DIMENSIONS

Bracelet, 8 inches (20.3 cm) long

Ring, ¾ inch (1.9 cm) diameter

DIFFICULTY LEVEL

Advanced

Flowers are the theme of this matched set. The triangle stitch is a three-sided version of the traditional RAW stitch and is perfect for making circular motifs such as these.

Bracelet

1 Cut and condition a length of thread you are comfortable working with. Thread a needle onto one end. String one size 11 seed bead and pass through it again to temporarily secure it. This will serve as the stop bead. Position it approximately 8 inches (20.3 cm) from the far end of your thread. This will be used later to attach your clasp. String one E and slide it down to the stop bead.

2 String one F, one A, one F, one A, and one F. Pass through one E to create a triangle.

3 Continue to pass through one F, one A, and one F in the new triangle.

4 String five Fs. Pass through the F from the triangle to form a circle. Continue to pass through the next F in the circle.

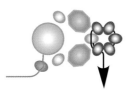

5 String one A, one F, and one E. Pass through one F and one A from the last triangle to create a new triangle. Continue to pass through the F you were originally coming out of and the next F in the circle.

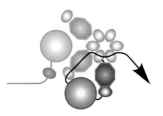

6 Repeat step 5 three times to add three new triangles.

7 Pass through one A and one F from the first triangle. String one E. Pass through one F and one A from the last triangle to create the sixth triangle. At this point, your blossom will begin to puff up a little. This is the desired result. Avoid pressing your blossom flat.

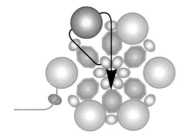

8 In the new triangle, pass through one F, one A, one F, and one E.

9 Pass through all six Es and pull tight enough so that the blossom puffs up. *This is optional, but tie one half-hitch knot after passing through the six Es to secure your tightly woven blossom and prevent it from flattening.* Continue to pass through two Es so that you are exiting out of the opposite side of where you started from. One blossom is finished!

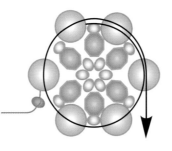

10 Repeat steps 2 to 9 to make a new blossom. This time, change the color of the blossom to Bs instead of As.

11 Repeat steps 2 to 9 to make a new blossom. This time, change the color of the blossom to Cs instead of Bs.

12 Repeat steps 2 to 9 to make a new blossom. This time, change the color of the blossom to Ds instead of Cs.

13 Continue to repeat steps 2 to 12, making new blossoms and changing the color for each new blossom. Stop when you're 1 inch (2.5 cm) from reaching your desired length. This is because the clasp will add length to your bracelet. (The version shown here contains 17 blossoms.)

14 String three Fs and one clasp end. Pass back down through one F. String two Fs. Pass through the E you were originally coming out

of to form a triangle. Pass through all the beads and the clasp end in the triangle again to reinforce the attachment.

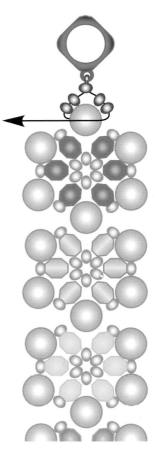

15 Pass through a few beads. Finish off the thread.

16 Remove the stop bead. Thread a needle onto the other end. Repeat steps 14 to 15 to attach the other half of the clasp and finish off the other end.

Your bracelet is finished—now on to the ring.

Ring

1 Cut and condition 1½ yards (1.4 m) of thread. Thread a needle onto one end. String one size 11° seed bead to serve as a stop bead and pass through it again to temporarily secure it. Slide the stop bead approximately 6 inches (15.2 cm) from the far end. String one E and slide it down to the stop bead.

2 String one F, one E, three Fs, one E, and one F. Pass through the E you were originally coming out of to form a square.

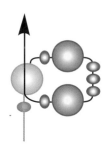

3 String two Fs, one C, and one F. Skip over one F and one E and pass through the three Fs.

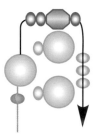

4 String one F. Pass through one C. String two Fs. Pass through the E you were originally coming out of to complete the embellishment over the square.

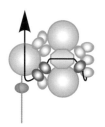

5 Repeat steps 2 to 9 from the Bracelet instructions to make one blossom. Use the D beads instead of the As.

6 Repeat steps 2 to 4 from the Ring instructions to add an embellished square. In the new square, continue to pass through one F, one E, and three Fs.

7 To start the ring band, string five Fs. Pass through the three Fs from the last square to create a new square. In the new square, continue to pass through four Fs.

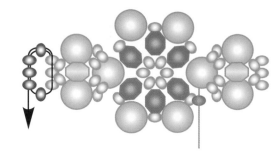

8 String five Fs. Pass through the middle three Fs from the last square to create a new square. In the new square, continue to pass through four Fs.

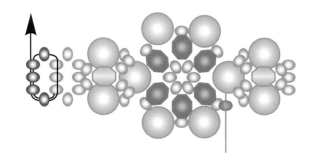

9 Continue to repeat step 7 to 8 from the Ring instructions until the band is long enough to wrap around your finger to meet the other side of the ring.

10 String one F. Pass through the three Fs on the other end of the ring to connect. String one F. Pass through the middle three Fs from the last square to complete the connection.

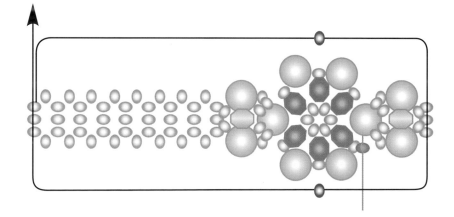

11 Use the remaining thread to pass through the beads in the connection and throughout the band to reinforce it. Finish off the thread. Remove the stop bead. Thread a needle onto the tail end. Finish off the thread.

8

beaded beads

One of my favorite uses of RAW is making little sparkling beaded beads. This chapter's projects incorporate everything you've learned in the previous chapters, primarily *Chapter 6: Going Tubular*. After all, beaded beads are just short beaded tubes.

For these types of projects, it's crucial to keep good tension. If you're a tight beader, then you will excel at beaded beads. If your bead tension is a little loose, coat your thread with beeswax or microcrystalline wax to help the beads stick together and achieve a firmer beaded bead.

Use these beads as you would any other beautiful bead. Beaded beads are a great way to incorporate wire and chain into a design! String them with other beads onto flexible beading wire, knot them onto silk cord, or wire wrap them onto chain for a contemporary feel.

lotus flower necklace & earrings

This design was inspired by the floral motifs on cloisonné beads. Crystals are framed with seed beads to create outlines shaped like the lovely petals of the lotus flower. Using wire and chain, you'll assemble nine elegant beaded beads into a long necklace. Make two more beads for the matching earrings.

Beaded Bead

1 Cut and condition 1 yard (91.4 cm) of thread. String one size 11° seed bead to serve as a stop bead. Pass through it again to temporarily secure it, then position the stop bead approximately 11 inches (27.9 cm) from the far end. String one A and slide it down to the stop bead.

2 String three As. Pass through the first A to form a square. Continue to pass through one A.

3 String three As. Pass through the A from the last square to form a new square. In the new square, pass through two As.

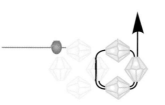

4 Repeat step 3 to add a third square.

5 String one A. Pass through the A from the first square. String one A. Pass through the A from the last square to complete the fourth square. Pass through one A in the new square.

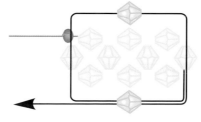

6 String one D. Pass through the next A.

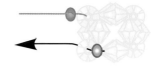

7 Repeat step 6 three times. Pass through the next D.

8 String three Bs, one C, and three Bs. Pass through the next D.

9 Repeat step 8 three times.

10 String two Bs, one D, and two Bs. Pass through the next D.

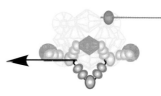

11 Repeat step 10 three times.

12 Pass through the next two Bs and one D.

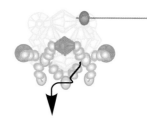

13 String one B. Pass through the next top D.

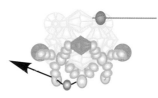

14 Repeat step 13 three times to form a circle.

15 Pass through the circle of beads again to reinforce it. Try to pull tight enough to eliminate any gaps of thread between the beads in the circle. Use the remaining thread to pass through the beads and tighten up any loose areas where you see gaps of thread. Finish off the thread.

16 Remove the stop bead. Thread a needle onto the tail end.

17 Repeat step 6 four times. Pass through the next D.

18 String three Bs. Pass through one C. String three Bs. Pass through the next D. One X embellishment over the square is complete.

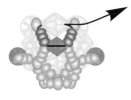

19 Repeat step 18 three more times.

20 Repeat steps 10 to 15 to finish the rest of the lotus bead. One beaded lotus bead is complete.

21 Repeat steps 1 to 20 to make 10 more lotus beads. You will need two lotus beads for a pair of earrings and nine for the necklace.

Necklace

22 Cut a 2½-inch (6.5 cm) piece of wire. With the chain-nose pliers, make a 90° bend approximately ¾ inch (1.9 cm) from the top.

23 With the round-nose pliers, grab the short wire up against the bend. Fold the wire up and over the top of the pliers. Adjust the pliers so that you can continue to fold the wire around the pliers until it crosses over the longer wire or stem. You should now have a loop centered on top of the stem like a lollipop.

24 Link the loop to a 1¼-inch (3.2 cm) piece of chain. Grab the loop with a pair of pliers. Grab the short wire with the chain-nose pliers and wrap it around the stem two or three times to create a short coil. Trim away the short wire with the flush cutters up against the coil. Use the chain-nose pliers to pinch the sharp edge into the coil.

25 String one C, one lotus bead, and one C onto the wire. With the tip of the chain-nose pliers, grab the stem right above the top bead. Fold the wire over the top of the pliers to make a 90° bend.

26 Repeat step 23 to make the loop.

27 Repeat step 24 to attach the loop to another piece of chain. When wrapping the short wire around the stem, wrap until you reach the top of the bead before trimming wire. One lotus bead link is complete.

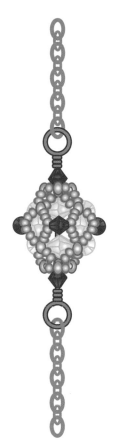

28 Cut a 2-inch (5.1 cm) piece of wire. With the chain-nose pliers, make a 90° bend approximately ¾ inch (1.9 cm) from the top.

29 Repeat steps 23 and 24 to make the loop and attach it to the chain.

30 String one D, one E, and one D. With the tip of the chain-nose pliers, grab the stem right above the top bead. Fold the wire over the top of the pliers to make a 90° bend.

31 Repeat steps 26 and 27 to complete the E bead link.

32 Repeat steps 22 to 31 eight more times to add length to the necklace. Use the ninth E bead link to connect the two ends of chain and finish the necklace.

Earrings

33 On the head pin, string one C, one lotus bead, and one C. With the tip of the chain-nose pliers, grab the stem right above the top bead. Fold the wire over the top of the pliers to make a 90° bend.

34 With the round-nose pliers, grab the short wire up against the bend. Fold the wire up and over the top of the pliers. Adjust the pliers so that you can continue to fold the wire around the pliers until it crosses over the longer wire or stem. You should now have a loop centered on top of the stem like a lollipop.

35 Grab the loop with a pair of pliers. Grab the short wire with the chain-nose pliers and wrap it around the stem a few times until you reach the top of the seed bead. Trim away the short wire up against the coil with the flush cutters. Use the chain-nose pliers to pinch the sharp edge into the coil. The lotus bead dangle is done.

36 Repeat steps 28 to 31 to add the E bead link. However, this time you will be linking to the lotus bead dangle instead of chain. The other loop of the link will link to nothing.

37 Now you will add a C bead link to the E bead link. This is similar to step 36, but instead of adding one D plus one E plus one D you will only be adding one C. The other loop will link to the earring finding. One earring is done.

38 Repeat steps 33 to 37 to make another earring to complete the pair.

lantern bead necklace

Like sunlight streaming through stained glass windows, light dances with these beaded beads. Each ornate lantern-shaped bead showcases glass beads framed in delicate seed beads. Make an ultra-chic double-strand necklace with 10 gorgeous beaded beads, some crystals, and chain.

YOU'LL NEED

240 fuchsia AB2X crystal bicones, 3 mm (A)

50 green gold-lined fire-polished glass beads, 4 mm (B)

Size 11° matte teal AB Japanese seed beads, 3 g (C)

Size 15° bronze Japanese seed beads, 3 g (D)

10 olivine AB crystal rounds, 8 mm (E)

17 inches (43.2 cm) of chain

4 open jump rings, 3 mm

Double-strand clasp

8 feet (2.4 m) of round wire, 24 to 26 gauge

FireLine, 6-pound test

Scissors

Thread conditioner (optional)

Size 12 beading needles

Plastic thread bobbin

Thread burner (optional)

Beading mat

Measuring tape

Chain-nose jewelry pliers

Round-nose jewelry pliers

Flush cutters

- - - - - - - - - - - - - - - -

DIMENSIONS

23¾ inches (18.4 cm) long

- - - - - - - - - - - - - - - -

DIFFICULTY LEVEL

Intermediate

Beaded Bead

1 Cut and condition 1 yard (91.4 cm) of thread. Wrap half of the thread onto a plastic thread bobbin. Thread a needle onto the other end. String one A and slide it down to the bobbin.

2 String one B, one A, and one B. Pass through the A you were originally coming out of to form a square. Continue to pass through one B.

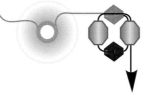

3 String one A, one B, and one A. Pass through the B from the last square to form a new square. In the new square, continue to pass through one A and one B.

4 Repeat step 3 two times to add two new squares.

5 String one A. Pass through the B from the first square. String one A. Pass through the B from the last square to complete the new square.

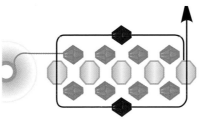

6 In the new square, continue to pass through one A, one B, and one A.

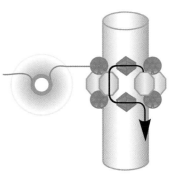

7 String one A, one C, and one A. Pass through the A you were originally coming out of to form a triangle. In the new triangle, pass down through one A.

8 String one C and one A. Pass through the next A. Pass through the A from the last triangle to form a new triangle. In the new triangle, pass through one C and one A. Pass through the next A.

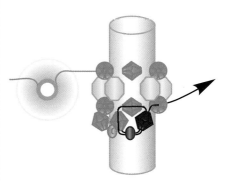

9 String one A and one C. Pass through the A from the last triangle to form a new triangle. In the new triangle, pass through two As.

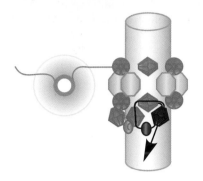

10 Repeat step 8 to add a new triangle.

11 Pass through the next A from the first triangle. String one C. Pass through the A from the last triangle to complete the new triangle. In the new triangle, pass through one A.

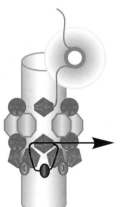

12 String one C. Pass through the next A.

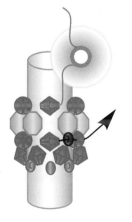

13 Repeat step 12 four times to go around the beaded bead.

14 Pass through one A and one C.

15 Pass through all five Cs to form a circle.

16 String one D. Pass through the next C.

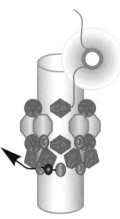

17 Repeat step 16 four times.

18 Pass through a few beads. Finish off the thread.

19 Unwind thread from the bobbin. Thread a needle onto the other end.

20 Repeat steps 7 to 13. Pass through the next C.

21 String three Ds, one C, and three Ds. Pass through one C. String three Ds, one C, and three Ds. Pass through the C you were originally coming out of to form a circle.

22 In the new circle, pass through three Ds and one C.

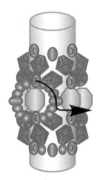

23 String three Ds. Pass through the next C. String three Ds, one C, and three Ds. Pass through one C. String three Ds. Pass through the C from the last circle to form a new circle.

24 In the new circle, pass through three Ds, one C, three Ds, and one C.

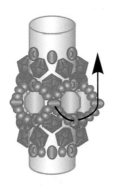

25 Repeat steps 23 and 24 two times to add two new circles.

26 String three Ds. Pass through one C. String three Ds. Pass through one C. String three Ds. Pass through one C. String three Ds. Pass through one C. This completes the new circle. In the new circle, continue to pass through three Ds and one C.

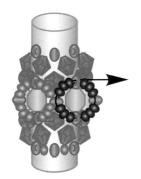

27 Pass through two As and one C so that you are exiting out of the top of the beaded bead.

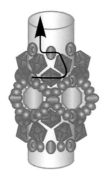

28 Repeat steps 15 to 18 to finish the beaded bead.

29 Repeat steps 1 to 28 to make a total of 10 beaded beads. Five beaded beads will be for the short strand, and five more beaded beads will be for the longer strand.

Necklace

30 Cut 22 pieces of chain each ¾ inch (1.9 cm) long. Tip: Measure and cut one piece of chain. Hang the piece of chain onto a needle or head pin. Hang the uncut chain onto the needle (or head pin) next to the cut piece. Use this piece as a guide for cutting the other pieces of chain. This method is easier than counting very small chain links to get the same length. However, if the chain links are big enough to see, then counting the links is easier.

31 Make the shorter strand first. Use an open jump ring to attach one piece of chain to the clasp end loop. To open the jump ring, simply twist it open holding the sides of the ring with a pair of chain-nose or flat-nose pliers. To close the jump ring, twist in the opposite direction.

32 Cut 3 inches (7.5 cm) of wire. With the chain-nose pliers, make a 90° bend approximately ¾ inch (1.9 cm) from the top.

33 With the round-nose pliers, grab the short wire up against the bend. Fold the wire up and over the top of the pliers. Readjust the pliers so that you can continue to fold the wire around the pliers until it crosses over the longer wire or stem. You should now have a loop centered on top of the stem like a lollipop.

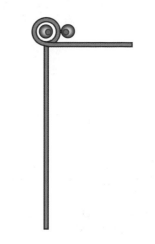

34 Link the loop to the piece of chain. Grab the loop with a pair of pliers. Grab the short wire with the chain-nose pliers and wrap it around the stem two or three times to create a short coil. Trim away the short wire with the flush cutters up against the coil. Use the chain-nose pliers to pinch the sharp edge into the coil.

35 String one A, one beaded bead, and one A.

36 With the tip of the chain-nose pliers, grab the stem right above the crystal. Fold the wire over the top of the pliers to make a 90° bend.

37 Repeat steps 33 and 34 to make a loop and link the loop to a new piece of chain. Be sure to continue wrapping down to the top of the crystal before trimming away excess wire.

38 Cut 2 inches (2.5 cm) of wire. With the chain-nose pliers, make a 90° bend approximately ¾ inch (1.9 cm) from the top. Refer to the figure in step 32 again.

39 Repeat steps 33 and 34 to make a loop and link it to the chain.

40 String one A. Repeat step 36 to make a 90° bend above the crystal. Repeat steps 33 and 34 to make a loop. There is nothing to link the loop to at this time. Be sure to continue wrapping down to the top of the crystal before trimming away the excess wire.

41 Repeat steps 38 and 39. This time, you will link the loop to the loop of the crystal link you just made in step 40.

42 String one E. Repeat step 36 to make a 90° bend above the crystal. Repeat steps 33 and 34 to make a loop. There is nothing to link the loop to at this time. Be sure to continue wrapping down to the top of the crystal before trimming away the excess wire.

43 Repeat steps 38 and 39. You will be linking the loop to the E bead link you just made. Repeat step 40 to add one A, make a 90° bend above the crystal, then make a loop and link that to a new piece of chain.

44 Continue to repeat steps 32 to 43 until you have linked a total of five beaded beads and used 10 pieces of chain. Repeat step 31 to attach the end to the other clasp end loop with a new open jump ring. The shorter strand is finished.

45 Now make the longer strand for your double-strand necklace. Repeat step 31 to attach a piece of chain to the other loop of the clasp end with an open jump ring.

46 Repeat steps 38 to 43 to attach an A bead link, an E bead link, an A bead link, and a piece of chain.

47 Repeat steps 32 to 37 to attach a beaded bead link and a piece of chain.

48 Continue to repeat steps 46 and 47 until you have linked a total of five beaded beads and used 12 pieces of chain. Repeat step 31 to attach the end to the other clasp end loop with a new open jump ring. The longer strand is finished.

Put it on. Wow, you look gorgeous!

variation

For this necklace, I made just one bead with a dangle hanging from it, and suspended them from a chain of gorgeous gemstones wired together.

dainty dots earrings

YOU'LL NEED

10 teal AB fire-polished glass beads, 4 mm (A)

Size 11° metallic light green Japanese seed beads, 1 g (B)

Size 15° light blue silver-lined Japanese seed beads, 1 g (C)

12 light gray opal AB2X crystal bicones, 3 mm (D)

Size 11° turquoise Japanese seed beads, 1.5 g (E)

2 light blue round beads, 4 mm (F)

2 head pins, 2 inches (5.1 cm)

1 pair of lever-back earring findings

FireLine, 6-pound test

Scissors

Thread conditioner (optional)

Size 12 beading needles

Plastic thread bobbin

Thread burner (optional)

Beading mat

Measuring tape

Chain-nose jewelry pliers

Round-nose jewelry pliers

Flush cutters

DIMENSIONS

2 inches (5.1 cm) long

DIFFICULTY LEVEL

Advanced

Here's a really fun pair of earrings. The color play and the dots give them a dash of whimsy.

Beaded Bead

1 Cut and condition 2½ yards (2.3 m) of thread. Wrap half of the thread onto a thread bobbin. Thread a needle onto the other end. String two Bs. Slide them next to the bobbin.

2 String one A, two Bs, and one A. Pass through the two Bs you were originally coming out of to form a square. Continue to pass through one A.

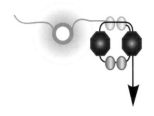

3 String two Bs, one A, and two Bs. Pass through the A from the last square to form a new square. Continue to pass through two Bs and one A.

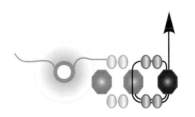

4 Repeat step 3 two times to add two new squares.

5 String two Bs. Pass through the A from the first square. String two Bs. Pass through the A from the last square to complete the fifth square. This creates a short tube.

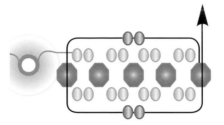

6 String two Cs, one D, and two Cs. Skip over two Bs. Pass through the other A of the same square.

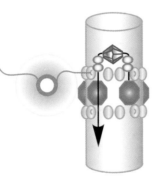

7 String two Cs. Pass through one D. String two Cs. Pass through the A on the other side of the same square. This creates an X embellishment over the square. In the same square, pass through two Bs and one A.

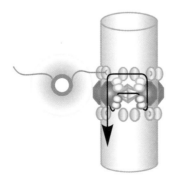

8 Repeat steps 6 and 7 four times, completing the X embellishment over the remaining four squares.

9 In that same square, pass through two Bs. You should be exiting out of the opposite side of the bobbin.

10 String five Es. Pass through the two Bs you are exiting out of to form a square. Continue to pass through two Es.

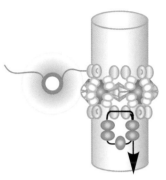

11 String three Es. Pass through the next two Bs. Pass through the two Es from the last square to form a new square. Continue to pass through three Es in the new square and the next two Bs.

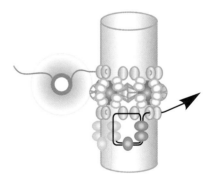

12 String three Es. Pass through the two Es from the last square to form a new square. In the new square, pass through two Bs and two Es.

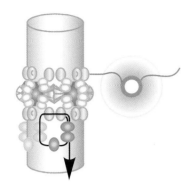

13 Repeat step 11 to add a new square.

14 Pass through two Es. String one E. Pass through the two Es from the last square to form a new square.

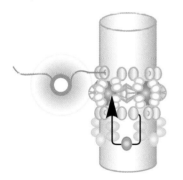

15 String two Cs, one B, and one C. Pass through the same two Es you were coming out of to form a triangle. In the triangle, pass through two Cs and one B.

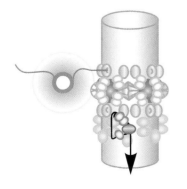

16 String one C. Pass through the two Es on the other side of the same square. String two Cs. Pass through one B. This creates a new triangle and completes the X embellishment over one square. In the new triangle, pass through one C and two Es.

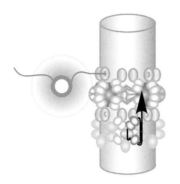

17 Repeat steps 15 and 16 four times to embellish the remaining four squares.

18 In the same square, pass through two Bs.

19 String one E. Pass through the next two Bs. Repeat this four more times, going completely around the beaded piece.

20 Pass through three Es in the square you are at. (This does not include the Es you added in the previous step.)

21 String one E, one B, and one E. Pass through the E you originally came out of to form a square. Continue to pass through the next E in the new square.

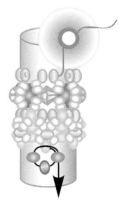

22 String one B and one E. Pass through the next E. Pass through the E from the last square to form a new square. In the new square, continue to pass through one B and one E. Pass through the next E.

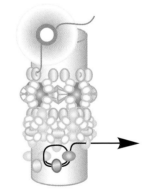

23 String one E and one B. Pass through the E from the last square to form a new square. In the new square, pass through two Es.

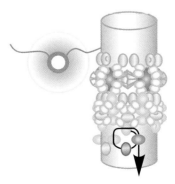

24 Repeat step 22 to add a new square.

25 Pass through one E from the first square. String one B. Pass through the E from the last square to form a new square. In the new square, continue to pass through two Es. Pass through the B in the next square.

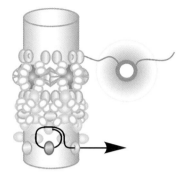

26 Pass through all five Bs and pull tight enough to eliminate any gaps between them.

27 String one E. Pass through the next B. Repeat this four more times, going completely around the beaded piece.

28 Pass through a few beads. Finish off the thread. Congratulations, half of the bead is finished!

29 Unwind thread from the bobbin. Thread a needle onto the other end. Repeat steps 10 to 28 to finish the other half of the beaded bead.

30 Repeat steps 1 to 29 to make a second beaded bead.

Assemble

1 On the head pin, string the following in order: one F, one beaded bead, and one D.

2 With the tip of the chain-nose pliers, grab the head pin right above the top bead. Fold the head pin over the top of the pliers to make a 90° bend.

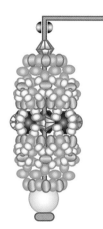

3 With the round-nose pliers, grab the short bent wire just at the bend. Fold the wire up and over the pliers. Adjust the position of the pliers so that it does not get in the way of the wire. Continue to fold the wire around the pliers to form a circle or loop. Stop when the wire crosses the straight part of the head pin.

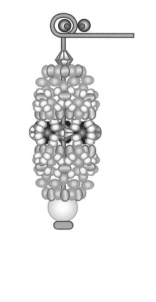

4 Grab the loop with a pair of pliers; with the chain-nose pliers, grab the shorter wire, and wrap it around the stem of the head pin a few times to create a coil up to the top bead.

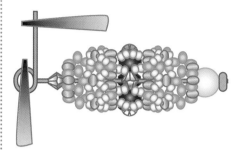

5 Trim away excess wire with the flush cutters. With the chain-nose pliers, pinch the short end into the coil to finish off any sharp edge. One dangle is complete.

6 With the chain-nose pliers, twist the link of the earring finding open. Link the finding to the loop of the dangle. With the pliers, twist the link closed to secure the connection. One earring is done.

7 Repeat steps 1 to 6 in the Assemble instructions to assemble another earring.

gallery

A

B

A GWEN L. FISHER
Cube Cluster Beaded Beads, 2011
Each bead, 2.5 cm in diameter
Glass and metal seed beads, glass beads;
RAW embellished with lace overlay
PHOTO BY ARTIST

B SMADAR GROSSMAN
Bollywood Glamour Necklace, 2009
41 cm long; each loop, 2.5 x 3 cm
Seed beads, crystals; RAW, peyote
stitch, brick stitch, embellished
PHOTO BY ARTIST

A

A GWEN L. FISHER
Icosahedral Cluster Beaded Art Object, 2005
2.7 x 1.8 x 0.7 cm
Glass and metal seed beads, quartz crystal;
RAW embellished with lace overlay
PHOTO BY ARTIST

B KELLY WIESE
Bohemian Bolo Necklace, 2011
45 x 2.5 x 1 cm
Seed beads, crystals;
embellished RAW
PHOTO BY ARTIST

B

C SUZANNE GOLDEN
Pastel Square Bracelets, 2011
Largest, 9 x 3.7 cm
Acrylic beads; RAW
PHOTO BY ROBERT DIAMANTE

D SABINE LIPPERT
Third Dimensional Piece, 2009
3 x 3 x 20 cm
Fire-polished beads, seed beads;
dimensional RAW
PHOTO BY ARTIST

E SABINE LIPPERT
Baroque Dimensional, 2010
2 x 2 x 20 cm
Fire-polished beads, glass pearls, seed beads,
drops; embellished dimensional RAW
PHOTO BY ARTIST

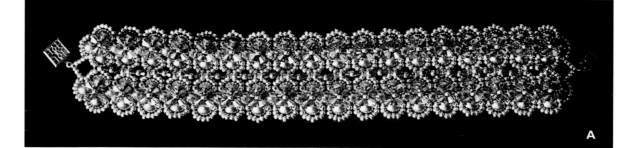

A JULIE MOORE TANKSLEY
The Contessa, 2009
1.3 x 3.8 x 20.3 cm
Glass pearls, crystal bicones, seed beads;
RAW with embellishments
PHOTO BY IMAGES BY BECKI

B DIANE FITZGERALD
Crystal Garden Necklace, 2011
45 x 1.3 cm
Crystal bicones, fire-polished round
beads, charlottes, gold, vermeil, fold-
over clasps, cubic zirconia; embellished
diagonal RAW
PHOTO BY ARTIST

C JULIE MOORE TANKSLEY
Art Deco Cross, 2009
1.3 x 5.7 x 5.7 cm
Glass pearls, crystal bicones, seed beads;
RAW with layering and embellishments
PHOTO BY IMAGES BY BECKI

D RACHEL NELSON-SMITH
Chiclets, 2011
5.1 x 19 cm
Seed beads, sterling silver, crystal,
nylon; RAW, peyote
PHOTO BY ARTIST

E RACHEL NELSON-SMITH
Atlas, 2011
6.4 x 19 cm
Sterling silver, crystal, nylon; RAW,
peyote
PHOTO BY ARTIST

F HUIB PETERSEN
Honky-Tonk, 1999
17.8 x 4.4 x 1.3 cm
Seed beads; RAW
PHOTO BY ARTIST

A DAENG WEAVER
Gold Bangle, 2011
7.6 cm in diameter
Seed beads, wrap-around vinyl tube,
multicolored sapphire; RAW
PHOTO BY ARTIST

B DAENG WEAVER
The Waves, 2011
19.1 cm long
Seed beads, turquoise, pearls,
tourmaline; RAW, circular peyote
PHOTO BY ARTIST

E

C HUIB PETERSEN
Triads, 2003
50.8 x 2.5 x 1.9 cm
Seed beads, blue jasper donut; RAW
PHOTO BY ARTIST

D HUIB PETERSEN
Celtic Basket Weave, 2002
50.8 x 3.8 x 1.3 cm
Seed beads; RAW
PHOTO BY ARTIST

E LAURA SHEA
Large Window Bead—Floral Version 1, 2009
3.2 cm in diameter
Crystal, monofilament; angle stitching
embellished with RAW
PHOTO BY DICK KAPLAN

A

Berry Glitz, 2011
21.5 x 1.3 x 1.3 cm
Seed beads, crystals, glass pearls,
pewter clasp; right angle weave
PHOTO BY STEWART O'SHIELDS

B

RAW Chic, 2009
19 x 1.5 x 1 cm
Seed beads, glass pearls, pewter clasp,
crystals; right angle weave
PHOTO BY STEWART O'SHIELDS

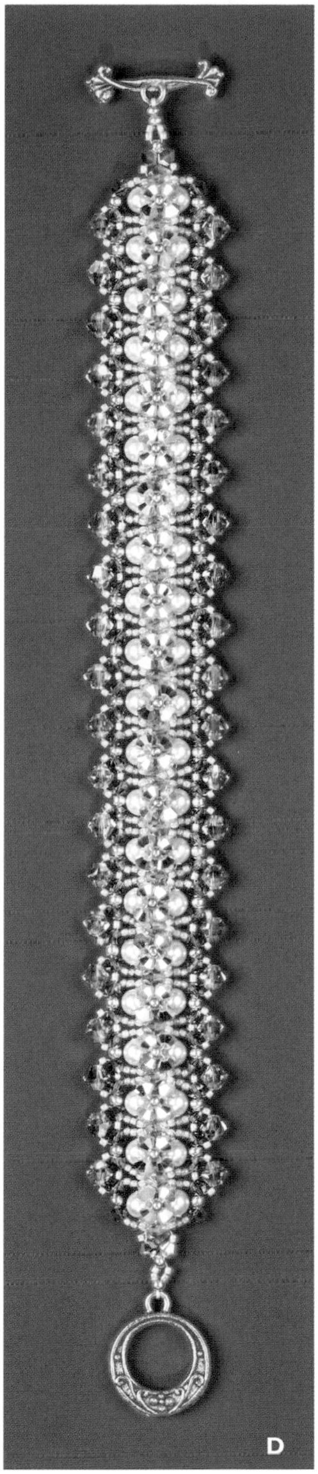

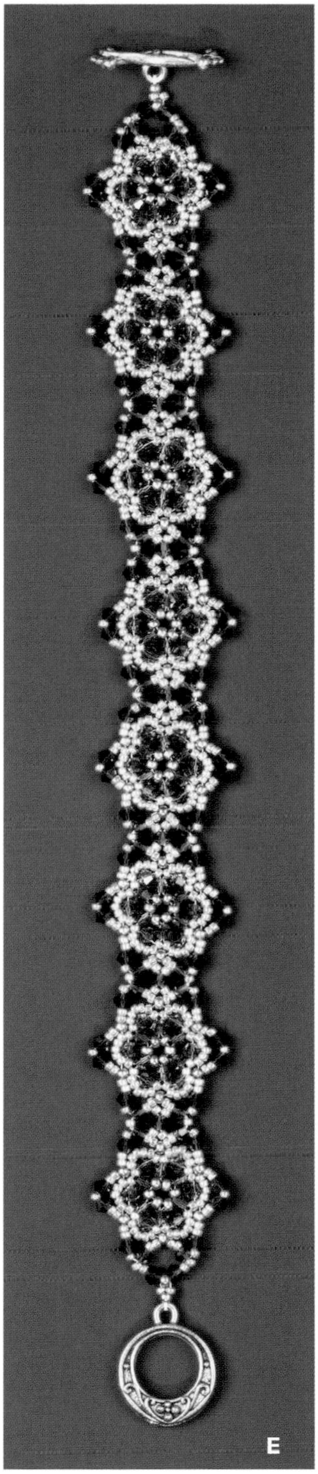

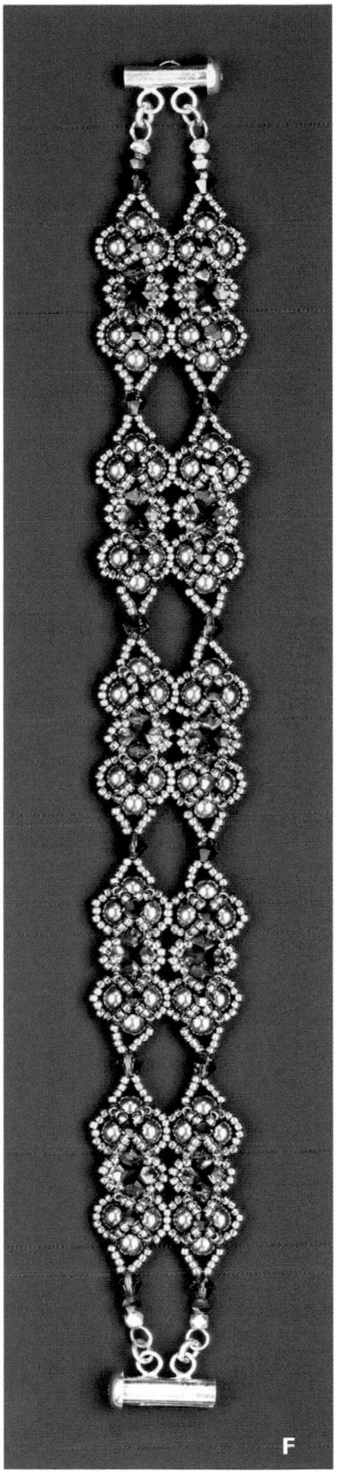

C

Marquis Mystery, 2011
17 × 3.5 × 0.5 cm
Seed beads, crystals, gold-plated clasp; right angle weave
PHOTO BY STEWART O'SHIELDS

D

Dazzle-licious, 2010
19.5 × 2.3 × 0.5 cm
Seed beads, glass pearls, crystals, pewter clasp; right angle weave
PHOTO BY STEWART O'SHIELDS

E

Starlight Flowers, 2010
20.5 × 2.5 × 0.3 cm
Seed beads, crystals, pewter clasp; right angle weave
PHOTO BY STEWART O'SHIELDS

F

Tiny Embraces, 2008
18.5 × 2 × 0.5 cm
Seed beads, glass pearls, crystals, silver beads, sterling silver clasp; right angle weave
PHOTO BY STEWART O'SHIELDS

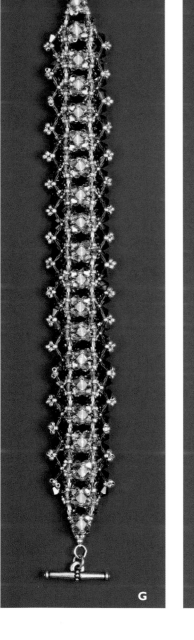

G

Moonlight Roses, 2007
19.5 x 2.3 x 0.5 cm
Seed beads, crystals, pewter
clasp; right angle weave
PHOTO BY STEWART O'SHIELDS

H

Serafina, 2009
18 x 3 x 0.4 cm
Seed beads, crystals, sterling
silver clasp; right angle weave
PHOTO BY STEWART O'SHIELDS

I

El Santiago, 2009
18.5 x 2.8 x 0.5 cm
Seed beads, glass pearls,
crystals, pewter clasp; right
angle weave
PHOTO BY STEWART O'SHIELDS

J

Cherry Blossoms, 2010
19 x 2 x 0.8 cm
Seed beads, glass pearls,
crystals; right angle weave
PHOTO BY STEWART O'SHIELDS

About the Author

Mabeline Gidez has been creating distinctive, handcrafted jewelry since 1996. In addition to crafting her own exclusive line of beaded finery, she also teaches jewelry-making classes at a number of popular Southern California bead shops and at the Bead&Button Show.

Mabeline has made several guest appearances on *The Carol Duvall Show* on HGTV and DIY Network. She recently provided custom silver earrings to two popular ABC shows, *The Bachelor* and *The Bachelorette*.

With a bachelor's degree in graphic design, Mabeline incorporates her knowledge of design and color theory into her work. She sells instructions for jewelry, as well as beading kits, on her website, www.mabelinedesigns.com.

Acknowledgments

Beading is a journey that has led me to find new friends, beautiful beads, and rediscover the beauty of this world. I am very fortunate to have so much support in pursuit of my beaded art.

First of all, I want to thank my family for all of their support and words of encouragement they have given me throughout the years. I am especially grateful to my husband, Dan. He is my source of motivation, my inner strength, my technical guru, and my human alarm clock to help me get out of bed on time.

Thank you to Gayle Joy for all of your help and bead expertise. You gave me my first shot at teaching a bead class. You were also the one who helped me get all the supplies I needed when I was making my own wedding jewelry. I shudder to think where I would be now if I had not found you.

To my two dearest friends, Evette Potts and Dianna Mooses. By knowing you both, I have grown so

much as an artist and as a human being. When I needed you, both of you were always there to support me and advise me. Both of you have been a constant source of creative inspiration!

This book wouldn't be possible without the talents of Nathalie Mornu, Bonnie Brooks, Dawn Dillingham, Hannah Doyle, and the rest of the talented staff at Lark Jewelry & Beading. You held my hand and guided me through this process and I am forever grateful.

Lastly, I want to thank all of the beaders who have believed in me, encouraged me, and supported my artistic endeavors by taking my classes and purchasing my instructions. Without you I wouldn't be able to put food on the table! I am always in awe of your creative vision and how you breathe new life into my designs with interesting color palettes and beautiful alterations. You (and beads) fuel my passion to bead!

Index

Gallery Contributors